W9-CIQ-382

Drucker in the
Harvard Business Review

DRUCKER IN THE *HARVARD BUSINESS REVIEW*

A Harvard Business Review Paperback

Harvard Business Review paperback No. 90033

ISBN 0-87584-289-5

The *Harvard Business Review* articles in this collection are
available as individual reprints. Discounts apply to quantity
purchases. For information and ordering contact Operations
Department, Harvard Business School Publishing Division,
Boston, MA 02163. Telephone: (617) 495-6192, 9 a.m. to 5
p.m. Eastern Standard Time, Monday through Friday. Fax:
(617) 495-6985, 24 hours a day.

© 1964, 1967, 1969, 1974, 1984, 1985, 1988, 1989, 1990, 1991
by the President and Fellows of Harvard College.

Editor's Note: Some articles in this book may have been written before authors and editors began to take into consideration the role of women in management. We hope the archaic
usage representing all managers as male does not detract from
the usefulness of the collection.

All rights reserved. No part of this book may be reproduced,
stored in a retrieval system, or transmitted, in any form or by
any means, electronic, mechanical, photocopying, recording,
or otherwise without the prior written permission of the
copyright holder.
Printed in the United States of America by Harvard
University, Office of the University Publisher.
93 92 91   5 4 3 2 1

Contents

Four concepts show us how the factory of 1999 must be built and managed.

The Emerging Theory of Manufacturing

by Peter F. Drucker

Japanese plants turn out two or three times more cars per worker than U.S. or European plants.

We cannot build it yet. But already we can specify the "postmodern" factory of 1999. Its essence will not be mechanical, though there will be plenty of machines. Its essence will be conceptual—the product of four principles and practices that together constitute a new approach to manufacturing.

Each of these concepts is being developed separately, by different people with different starting points and different agendas. Each concept has its own objectives and its own kinds of impact. Statistical Quality Control is changing the social organization of the factory. The new manufacturing accounting lets us make production decisions as business decisions. The "flotilla," or module, organi-

zation of the manufacturing process promises to combine the advantages of standardization and flexibility. Finally, the systems approach embeds the physical process of making things, that is, manufacturing, in the economic process of business, that is, the business of creating value.

As these four concepts develop, they are transforming how we think about manufacturing and how we manage it. Most manufacturing people in the United States now know we need a new theory of

Peter F. Drucker is the Clarke Professor of Social Science and Management at the Claremont Graduate School in Claremont, California. His most recent book is The New Realities *(Harper & Row, 1989).*

manufacturing. We know that patching up old theories has not worked and that further patching will only push us further behind. Together these concepts give us the foundation for the new theory we so badly need.

The most widely publicized of these concepts, Statistical Quality Control (SQC), is actually not new at all. It rests on statistical theory formulated 70 years ago by Sir Ronald Fisher. Walter Shewhart, a Bell Laboratories physicist, designed the original version of SQC in the 1930s for the zero-defects mass production of complex telephone exchanges and telephone sets. During World War II, W. Edwards Deming and Joseph Juran, both

former members of Shewhart's circle, separately developed the versions used today.

The Japanese owe their leadership in manufacturing quality largely to their embrace of Deming's precepts in the 1950s and 1960s. Juran too had great impact in Japan. But U.S. industry ignored their contributions for 40 years and is only now converting to SQC, with companies such as Ford, General Motors, and Xerox among the new disciples. Western Europe also has largely ignored the concept. More important, even SQC's most successful practitioners do not thoroughly understand what it really does. Generally, it is considered a production tool. Actually, its greatest impact is on the factory's social organization.

By now, everyone with an interest in manufacturing knows that SQC is a rigorous, scientific method of identifying the quality and productivity that can be expected from a given production process in its current form so that control of both attributes can be built into the process itself. In addition, SQC can instantly spot malfunctions and show where they occur—a worn tool, a dirty spray gun, an overheating furnace. And because it can do this with a small sample, malfunctions are reported almost immediately, allowing machine operators to correct problems in real time. Further, SQC quickly identifies the impact of any change on the performance of the entire process. (Indeed, in some applications developed by Deming's Japanese disciples, computers can simulate the effects of a proposed change in advance.) Finally, SQC identifies where, and often how, the quality and productivity of the entire process can be continuously improved. This used to be called the "Shewhart Cycle" and then the "Deming Cycle"; now it is *kaizen*, the Japanese term for continuous improvement.

But these engineering characteristics explain only a fraction of SQC's results. Above all, they do not explain the productivity gap between Japanese and U.S. factories. Even after adjusting for their far greater reliance on outside suppliers, Toyota, Honda, and Nissan turn out two or three times more cars per worker than comparable U.S. or European plants do. Building quality into the process accounts for no more than one-third of this difference. Japan's major productivity gains are the result of social changes brought about by SQC.

The Japanese employ proportionately more machine operators in direct production work than Ford or GM. In fact, the introduction of SQC almost always increases the number of machine operators. But this increase is offset many times over by the sharp drop in the number of nonoperators: inspectors, above all, but also the people who do not *do* but *fix*, like repair crews and "fire fighters" of all kinds.

In U.S. factories, especially mass-production plants, such nonoperating, blue-collar employees substantially outnumber operators. In some plants, the ratio is two to one. Few of these workers are needed under SQC. Moreover, first-line supervisors also are gradually eliminated, with only a handful of trainers taking their place. In other words, not only does SQC make it possible for machine operators to be in control of their work, it makes such control almost mandatory. No one else has the hands-on knowledge needed to act effectively on the information that SQC constantly feeds back.

By aligning information with accountability, SQC resolves a heretofore irresolvable conflict. For more than a century, two basic approaches to manufacturing have prevailed, especially in the United States. One is the engineering approach pioneered by Frederick Winslow Taylor's "scientific management." The other is the "human relations" (or "human resources") approach developed before World War I by Andrew Carnegie, Julius Rosenwald of Sears Roebuck, and Hugo Münsterberg, a Harvard psychologist. The two approaches have always been considered antitheses, indeed, mutually exclusive. In SQC, they come together.

Taylor and his disciples were just as determined as Deming to build quality and productivity into the manufacturing process. Taylor asserted that his "one

> ## Most U.S. quality circles of the last 20 years have failed because they lacked rigorous and reliable feedback.

right way" guaranteed zero-defects quality; he was as vehemently opposed to inspectors as Deming is today. So was Henry Ford, who claimed that his assembly line built quality and productivity into the process (though he was otherwise untouched by Taylor's scientific management and probably did not even know about it). But without SQC's rigorous methodology, neither scientific management nor the assembly line could actually deliver built-in process control. With all their successes, both scientific management and the assembly line had to fall back on massive inspection, to fix problems rather than eliminate them.

The human-relations approach sees the knowledge and pride of line workers as the greatest resource for controlling and improving quality and productivity. It too has had important successes. But without the kind of information SQC provides, you cannot readily distinguish productive activity from busy-ness. It is also hard to tell whether a proposed modification will truly improve the process or simply make things look better in one corner, only to make them worse overall.

Quality circles, which were actually invented and widely used in U.S. industry during World War II, have been successful in Japan because they came in after SQC had been established. As a result, both the quality circle and management have objective information about the effects of workers' suggestions. In contrast, most U.S. quality circles of the last 20 years have failed despite great enthusiasm, especially on the part of workers. The reason? They were established without SQC, that is, without rigorous and reliable feedback.

A good many U.S. manufacturers have built quality and productivity into their manufacturing processes without SQC and yet with a minimum of inspection and fixing. Johnson & Johnson is one such example. Other companies have successfully put machine operators in control of the manufacturing process without instituting SQC. IBM long ago replaced all first-line supervisors with a handful of "managers" whose main task is to train, while Herman Miller achieves zero-defects quality and high productivity through continuous training and productivity-sharing incentives.

But these are exceptions. In the main, the United States has lacked the methodology to build quality and productivity into the manufacturing process. Similarly, we have lacked the methodology to move responsibility for the process and control of it to the machine operator, to put into practice what the mathematician Norbert Wiener called the "human use of human beings."

SQC makes it possible to attain both traditional aspirations: high quality and productivity on the one hand, work worthy of human beings on the other. By fulfilling the aims of the traditional factory, it provides the capstone for the edifice of twentieth century manufacturing that Frederick Taylor and Henry Ford designed.

Bean counters do not enjoy a good press these days. They are blamed for all the ills that afflict U.S. manufacturing. But the bean counters will have the last laugh. In the factory of 1999, manufacturing accounting will play as big a role as it ever did and probably even a bigger one. But the beans will be counted differently. The new manufacturing accounting, which might more accurately be called "manufacturing economics," differs radically from traditional cost accounting in its basic concepts. Its aim is to integrate manufacturing with business strategy.

Manufacturing cost accounting (cost accounting's rarely used full name) is the third leg of the stool – the other legs being scientific management and the assembly line – on which modern manufacturing industry rests. Without cost accounting, these two could never have become fully effective. It too is American in origin. Developed in the 1920s by General Motors, General Electric, and Western Electric (AT&T's manufacturing arm), the new cost accounting, not technology, gave GM and GE the competitive edge that made them worldwide industry leaders. Following World War II, cost accounting became a major U.S. export.

But by that time, cost accounting's limitations also were becoming apparent. Four are particularly important. First, cost accounting is based on the realities of the 1920s, when direct, blue-collar labor accounted for 80% of all manufacturing costs other than raw materials. Consequently, cost accounting equates "cost" with direct labor costs. Everything else is "miscellaneous," lumped together as overhead.

These days, however, a plant in which direct labor costs run as high as 25% is a rare exception. Even in automobiles, the most labor intensive of the major industries, direct labor costs in up-to-date plants (such as those the Japanese are building in the United States and some of the new Ford plants) are down to 18%. And 8% to 12% is fast becoming the industrial norm. One large manufacturing company with a labor-intensive process, Beckman Instruments, now considers labor costs "miscellaneous." But typically, cost accounting systems are still based on direct labor costs that are carefully, indeed minutely, accounted for. The remaining costs – and that can mean 80% to 90% – are allocated by ratios that everyone knows are purely arbitrary and totally misleading: in direct proportion to a product's labor costs, for example, or to its dollar volume.

Second, the benefits of a change in process or in method are primarily defined in terms of labor cost savings. If other savings are considered at all, it is usually on the basis of the same arbitrary allocation by which costs other than direct labor are accounted for.

Even more serious is the third limitation, one built into the traditional cost accounting system. Like a sundial, which shows the hours when the sun shines but gives no information on a cloudy day or at night, traditional cost accounting measures only the costs of producing. It ignores the costs of nonproducing, whether they result from machine downtime or from quality defects that require scrapping or reworking a product or part.

Standard cost accounting assumes that the manufacturing process turns out good products 80% of the time. But we now know that even with the best SQC, nonproducing time consumes far more than 20% of total production time. In some plants, it accounts for 50%. And nonproducing time costs as much as producing time does – in wages, heat, lighting, interest, salaries, even raw materials. Yet the traditional system measures none of this.

Finally, manufacturing cost accounting assumes the factory is an isolated entity. Cost savings in the factory are "real." The rest is "speculation" – for ex-

> **Traditional cost accounting can hardly justify a product *improvement*, let alone an *innovation*.**

ample, the impact of a manufacturing process change on a product's acceptance in the market or on service quality. GM's plight since the 1970s illustrates the problem with this assumption. Marketing people were unhappy with top management's decision to build all car models, from Chevrolet to Cadillac, from the same small number of bodies, frames, and engines. But the cost accounting model showed that such commonality would produce substantial labor cost savings. And so marketing's argument that GM cars would lose customer appeal as they looked more and more alike was brushed aside as speculation. In effect, traditional cost accounting can hardly justify a product *improvement*, let alone a product or process *innovation*. Automation, for instance, shows up as a cost but almost never as a benefit.

All this we have known for close to 40 years. And for 30 years, accounting scholars, government accountants, industry accountants, and accounting firms have worked hard to reform the system. They have made substantial improvements. But since the reform attempts tried to build on the traditional system, the original limitations remain.

What triggered the change to the new manufacturing accounting was the frustration of factory-automation equipment makers. The potential users, the people in the plants, badly wanted the new equipment. But top management could not be persuaded to spend the money on numerically controlled machine tools or robots that could rapidly change tools, fixtures, and molds. The benefits of automated equipment, we now know, lie primarily in the reduction of nonproducing time by improving quality (that is, getting it right the first time) and by sharply curtailing machine downtime in changing over from one model or product to another. But these gains cost accounting does not document.

Out of this frustration came Computer-Aided Manufacturing-International, or CAM-I, a cooperative effort by automation producers, multinational manufacturers, and accountants to develop a new cost accounting system. Started in 1986, CAM-I is just beginning to influence manufacturing practice. But already it has unleashed an intellectual revolution. The most exciting and innovative work in management today is found in accounting theory, with new concepts, new approaches, new methodology—even what might be called new economic philosophy—rapidly taking shape. And while there is enormous controversy over specifics, the lineaments of the new manufacturing accounting are becoming clearer every day.

As soon as CAM-I began its work, it became apparent that the traditional accounting system could not be reformed. It had to be replaced. Labor costs are clearly the wrong unit of measurement in manufacturing. But—and this is a new insight—so are all the other elements of production. The new measurement unit has to be time. The costs for a given period of time must be assumed to be fixed; there are no "variable" costs. Even material costs are more fixed than variable, since defective output uses as much material as good output does. The only thing that is both variable and controllable is how much time a given process takes. And "benefit" is whatever reduces that time. In one fell swoop, this insight eliminates the first three of cost accounting's four traditional limitations.

> In the new accounting,
> finished-goods inventory is a
> sunk cost, not an asset.

But the new cost concepts go even further by redefining what costs and benefits really are. For example, in the traditional cost accounting system, finished-goods inventory costs nothing because it does not absorb any direct labor. It is treated as an "asset." In the new manufacturing accounting, however, inventory of finished goods is a "sunk cost" (an economist's, not an accountant's, term). Stuff that sits in inventory does not earn anything. In fact, it ties down expensive money and absorbs time. As a result, its time costs are high. The new accounting measures these time costs against the benefits of finished-goods inventory (quicker customer service, for instance).

Yet manufacturing accounting still faces the challenge of eliminating the fourth limitation of traditional cost accounting: its inability to bring into the measurement of factory performance the impact of manufacturing changes on the total business—the return in the marketplace of an investment in automation, for instance, or the risk in not making an investment that would speed up production changeovers. The in-plant costs and benefits of such decisions can now be worked out with considerable accuracy. But the business consequences are indeed speculative. One can only say, "Surely, this should help us get more sales," or "If we don't do this, we risk falling behind in customer service." But how do you quantify such opinions?

Cost accounting's strength has always been that it confines itself to the measurable and thus gives objective answers. But if intangibles are brought into its equations, cost accounting will only raise more questions. How to proceed is thus hotly debated, and with good reason. Still, everyone agrees that these business impacts have to be integrated into the measurement of factory performance, that is, into manufacturing accounting. One way or another, the new accounting will force managers, both inside and outside the plant, to make manufacturing decisions as *business* decisions.

Henry Ford's epigram, "The customer can have any color as long as it's black," has entered American folklore. But few people realize what Ford meant: flexibility costs time and money, and the customer won't pay for it. Even fewer people realize that in the mid-1920s, the "new" cost accounting made it possible for GM to beat Ford by giving customers both colors and annual model changes at no additional cost.

By now, most manufacturers can do what GM learned to do roughly 70 years ago. Indeed, many go quite a bit further in combining standardization with flexibility. They can, for example, build a variety of end products from a fairly small number of standardized parts. Still, manufacturing people tend to think like Henry Ford: you can have either standardization at low cost or flexibility at high cost, but not both.

The factory of 1999, however, will be based on the premise that you not only *can* have both but also *must* have both—and at low cost. But to achieve this, the factory will have to be structured quite differently.

Today's factory is a battleship. The plant of 1999 will be a "flotilla," consisting of modules centered either around a stage in the production process or around a number of closely related operations. Though overall command and control will still exist, each module will have its own

command and control. And each, like the ships in a flotilla, will be maneuverable, both in terms of its position in the entire process and its relationship to other modules. This organization will give each module the benefits of standardization and, at the same time, give the whole process greater flexibility. Thus it will allow rapid changes in design and product, rapid response to market demands, and low-cost production of "options" or "specials" in fairly small batches.

No such plant exists today. No one can yet build it. But many manufacturers, large and small, are moving toward the flotilla structure: among them are some of Westinghouse's U.S. plants, Asea Brown Boveri's robotics plant in Sweden, and several large printing plants, especially in Japan.

The biggest impetus for this development probably came from GM's failure to get a return on its massive (at least $30 billion and perhaps $40 billion) investment in automation. GM, it seems, used the new machines to improve its existing process, that is, to make the assembly line more efficient. But the process instead became less flexible and less able to accomplish rapid change.

Meanwhile, Japanese automakers and Ford were spending less and attaining more flexibility. In these plants, the line still exists, but it is discontinuous rather than tightly tied together. The new equipment is being used to speed changes, for example, automating changeovers of jigs, tools, and fixtures. So the line has acquired a good bit of the flexibility of traditional batch production without losing its standardization. Standardization and flexibility are thus no longer an either-or proposition. They are – as indeed they must be – melded together.

This means a different balance between standardization and flexibility, however, for different parts of the manufacturing process. An "average" balance across the plant will do nothing very well. If imposed throughout the

line, it will simply result in high rigidity and big costs for the entire process, which is apparently what happened at GM. What is required is a reorganization of the process into modules, each with its own optimal balance.

Moreover, the relationships between these modules may have to change whenever the product, process, or distribution changes. Switching from selling heavy equipment to leasing it, for instance, may drastically change the ratio between finished-product output and spare-parts output. Or a fairly minor model change may alter the sequence in which major parts are assembled into the finished product. There is nothing very new in this, of course. But under the traditional line structure, such changes are ignored, or they take forever to accomplish. With competition intensifying and product life cycles shortening all the time, such changes cannot be ignored, and they have to be done fast. Hence the flotilla's modular organization.

But this organization requires more than a fairly drastic change in the factory's physical structure. It requires, above all, different communication and information. In the traditional plant, each sector and department reports separately upstairs. And it reports what upstairs has asked for. In the factory of 1999, sectors and departments will have to think through what information they owe to whom and what information they need from whom. A good deal of this information will flow sideways and across department lines, not upstairs. The factory of 1999 will be an information network.

Consequently, all the managers in a plant will have to know and understand the entire process, just as the destroyer commander has to know and understand the tactical plan of the entire flotilla. In the factory of 1999, managers will have to

think and act as team members, mindful of the performance of the whole. Above all, they will have to ask: What do the people running the other modules need to know about the characteristics, the capacity, the plans, and the performance of *my* unit? And what, in turn, do we in my module need to know about theirs?

The last of the new concepts transforming manufacturing is systems design, in which the whole of manufacturing is seen as an integrated process that converts materials into goods, that is, into economic satisfactions.

Marks & Spencer, the British retail chain, designed the first such system in the 1930s. Marks & Spencer designs and tests the goods (whether textiles or foods) it has decided to sell. It designates one manufacturer to make each product under contract. It works with the manufacturer to produce the right merchandise with the right quality at the right price. Finally, it organizes just-in-time delivery of the finished products to its stores. The entire process is governed by a meticulous forecast as to when the goods will move off store shelves and into customers' shopping bags. In the last ten years or so, such systems management has become common in retailing.

> Henry Ford did not build a system at River Rouge. He built an unwieldy monster.

Though systems organization is still rare in manufacturing, it was actually first attempted there. In the early 1920s, when the Model T was in its full glory, Henry Ford decided to control the entire process of making and moving all the supplies and parts needed by his new plant, the gigantic River Rouge. He built his own steel mill and glass plant. He founded plantations in Brazil to grow rubber for tires. He bought the railroad that brought supplies to River Rouge and carried away the finished cars. He even toyed with the idea of building his own service centers nationwide and staffing them with mechanics trained in Ford-owned schools. But Ford conceived of all this as a financial edifice held together by ownership. Instead of building a system, he built a conglomerate, an unwieldy monster that was expensive, unmanageable, and horrendously unprofitable.

In contrast, the new manufacturing system is not "controlled" at all. Most of its parts are independent—independent suppliers at one end, customers at the other. Nor is it plant centered, as Ford's organization was. The new system sees the plant as little more than a wide place in the manufacturing stream. Planning and scheduling start with shipment to the final customer, just as they do at Marks & Spencer. Delays, halts, and redundancies have to be designed into the system—a warehouse here, an extra supply of parts and tools there, a stock of old products that are no longer being made but are still occasionally demanded by the market. These are necessary imperfections in a continuous flow that is governed and directed by information.

What has pushed American manufacturers into such systems design is the trouble they encountered when they copied Japan's just-in-time methods for supplying plants with materials and parts. The trouble could have been predicted, for the Japanese scheme is founded in social and logistic conditions unique to that country and unknown in the United States. Yet the shift seemed to American manufacturers a matter of procedure, indeed, almost trivial. Company after company found, however, that just-in-time delivery of supplies and parts created turbulence throughout their plants. And while no one could figure out what the problem was, the one thing that became clear was that with just-in-time deliveries, the plant no longer functions as a step-by-step process that begins at the receiving dock and ends when finished goods move into the shipping room. Instead, the plant must be redesigned from the end backwards and managed as an integrated flow.

Manufacturing experts, executives, and professors have urged such an approach for two or three decades now. And some industries, such as petroleum refining and large-scale construction, do practice it. But by and large, American and European manufacturing plants are neither systems designed nor systems managed. In fact, few companies have enough knowledge about what goes on in their plants to run them as systems. Just-in-time delivery, however, forces managers to ask systems questions: Where in the plant do we need redundancy? Where should we place the burden of adjustments? What costs should we incur in one place to minimize delay, risk, and vulnerability in another?

> Producing does not stop when the product leaves the factory. Distribution and service are integral parts of the process.

A few companies are even beginning to extend the systems concept of manufacturing beyond the plant and into the marketplace. Caterpillar, for instance, organizes its manufacturing to supply any replacement part anywhere in the world within 48 hours. But companies like this are still exceptions; they must become the rule. As soon as we define manufacturing as the process that converts things into economic satisfactions, it becomes clear that producing does not stop when the product leaves the factory. Physical distribution and product service are still part of the production process and should be integrated with it, coordinated with it, managed together with it. It is already widely recognized that servicing the product must be a major consideration during its design and production. By 1999, systems manufacturing will have an increasing influence on how we design and remodel plants and on how we manage manufacturing businesses.

Traditionally, manufacturing businesses have been organized "in series," with functions such as engineering, manufacturing, and marketing as successive steps. These days, that system is often complemented by a parallel team organization (Procter & Gamble's product management teams are a well-known example), which brings various functions together from the inception of a new product or process project. If manufacturing is a system, however, every decision in a manufacturing business becomes a manufacturing decision. Every decision should meet manufacturing's requirements and needs and in turn should exploit the strengths and capabilities of a company's particular manufacturing system.

When Honda decided six or seven years ago to make a new, upscale car for the U.S. market, the most heated strategic debate was not about design, performance, or price. It was about whether to distribute the Acura through Honda's well-established dealer network or to create a new market segment by building separate Acura dealerships at high cost and risk. This was a marketing issue, of course. But the decision was made by a team of design, engineering, manufacturing, and marketing people. And what tilted the balance toward the separate dealer network was a manufacturing consideration: the design for which independent distribution and service made most sense was the design that best utilized Honda's manufacturing capabilities.

Full realization of the systems concept in manufacturing is years away. It may not require a new Henry Ford. But it will certainly require very different management and very different managers. Every manager in tomorrow's manufacturing business will have to know and understand the manufacturing system. We might well adopt the Japanese custom of starting all new management people in the plant and in manufacturing jobs for the first few years of their careers. Indeed, we might go even further and require managers throughout the company to rotate into fac-

tory assignments throughout their careers—just as army officers return regularly to troop duty.

In the new manufacturing business, manufacturing is the integrator that ties everything together. It creates the economic value that pays for everything and everybody. Thus the greatest impact of the manufacturing systems concept will not be on the production process. As with SQC, its greatest impact will be on social and human concerns—on career ladders, for instance, or more important, on the transformation of *functional* managers into *business* managers, each with a specific role, but all members of the same production and the same cast. And surely, the manufacturing businesses of tomorrow will not be run by financial executives, marketers, or lawyers inexperienced in manufacturing, as so many U.S. companies are today.

There are important differences among these four concepts. Consider, for instance, what each means by "the factory." In SQC, the factory is a place where people work. In management accounting and the flotilla concept of flexible manufacturing, it is a place where work is being done—it makes no difference whether by people, by white mice, or

Caterpillar organizes its manufacturing to supply any part anywhere in the world within 48 hours.

by robots. In the systems concept, the factory is not a place at all; it is a stage in a process that adds economic value to materials. In theory, at least, the factory cannot and certainly should not be designed, let alone built, until the entire process of "making" –

> ## Understand the "making" process all the way to the final customer. Then design and build the factory.

all the way to the final customer – is understood. Thus defining the factory is much more than a theoretical or semantic exercise. It has immediate practical consequences on plant design, location, and size; on what activities are to be brought together in one manufacturing complex; even on how much and in what to invest.

Similarly, each of these concepts reflects a particular mind-set. To apply SQC, you don't have to think, you have to do. Management accounting concentrates on technical analysis, while the flotilla concept focuses on organization design and work flow. In the systems concept, there is great temptation to keep on thinking and never get to the doing. Each concept has its own tools, its own language, and addresses different people.

Nevertheless, what these four concepts have in common is far more important than their differences. Nowhere is this more apparent than in their assumption that the manufacturing process is a configuration, a whole that is greater than the sum of its parts. Traditional approaches all see the factory as a collection of individual machines and individual operations. The nineteenth century factory was an assemblage of machines. Taylor's scientific manage-

ment broke up each job into individual operations and then put those operations together into new and different jobs. "Modern" twentieth century concepts – the assembly line and cost accounting – define performance as the sum of lowest cost operations. But none of the new concepts is much concerned with performance of the parts. Indeed, the parts as such can only underperform. The process produces results.

Management also will reflect this new perspective. SQC is the most nearly conventional in its implications for managers, since it does not so much change their job as shift much of it to the work force. But even managers with no business responsibility (and under SQC, plant people have none) will have to manage with an awareness of business considerations well beyond the plant. And every manufacturing manager will be responsible for integrating people, materials, machines, and time. Thus every manufacturing manager ten years hence will have to learn and practice a discipline that integrates engineering, management of people, and business economics into the manufacturing process. Quite a few manufacturing people are doing this already, of course – though usually unaware that they are doing something new and different. Yet such a discipline has not been systematized and is still not taught in engineering schools or business schools.

These four concepts are synergistic in the best sense of this much-abused term. Together – but only together – they tackle the conflicts that have most troubled traditional, twentieth century mass-production plants: the conflicts between people and machines, time and money, standardization and flexibility, and functions and systems. The key is that every one of these concepts defines performance as productivity and conceives of manufacturing as the physical process that adds economic value to materials. Each tries to provide economic value in a different way. But they share the same theory of manufacturing.

Author's note: I wish to acknowledge gratefully the advice and criticism I received on this piece from Bela Gold and Joseph Maciariello, friends and colleagues at the Claremont Graduate School.

Reprint 90303

*The best management practice and most innovative
methods now come from the Girl Scouts and the Salvation Army.*

What Business Can Learn from Nonprofits

by Peter F. Drucker

The Girl Scouts, the Red Cross, the pastoral churches – our nonprofit organizations – are becoming America's management leaders. In two areas, strategy and the effectiveness of the board, they are practicing what most American businesses only preach. And in the most crucial area – the motivation and productivity of knowledge workers – they are truly pioneers, working out the policies and practices that business will have to learn tomorrow.

Few people are aware that the nonprofit sector is by far America's largest employer. Every other adult – a total of 80 million plus people – works as a volunteer, giving on average nearly five hours each week to one or several nonprofit organizations. This is equal to 10 million full-time jobs. Were volunteers paid, their wages, even at minimum rate, would amount to some $150 billion, or 5% of GNP. And volunteer work is changing fast. To be sure, what many do requires little skill or judgment: collecting in the neighborhood for the Community Chest one Saturday afternoon a year, chaperoning youngsters selling Girl Scout cookies door to door, driving old people to the doctor. But more and more volunteers are becoming "unpaid staff," taking over the professional and managerial tasks in their organizations.

Not all nonprofits have been doing well, of course. A good many community hospitals are in dire straits. Traditional churches and synagogues of all persuasions – liberal, conservative, evangelical, fundamentalist – are still steadily losing members. Indeed, the sector overall has not expanded in the last 10 or 15 years, either in terms of the money it raises (when adjusted for inflation) or in the number of vol-

> **The Salvation Army rehabilitates some 20,000 young criminals each year for a fraction of what it would cost to keep them in jail.**

unteers. Yet in its productivity, in the scope of its work and in its contribution to American society, the nonprofit sector has grown tremendously in the last two decades.

The Salvation Army is an example. People convicted to their first prison term in Florida, mostly very poor black or Hispanic youths, are now paroled into the Salvation Army's custody – about 25,000

Peter F. Drucker is the Marie Rankin Clarke Professor of Social Sciences and Management at the Claremont Graduate School, which has named its management center after him. His most recent book is The New Realities *(Harper & Row, 1989). This is Mr. Drucker's twenty-sixth article in HBR.*

each year. Statistics show that if these young men and women go to jail the majority will become habitual criminals. But the Salvation Army has been able to rehabilitate 80% of them through a strict work program run largely by volunteers. And the program costs a fraction of what it would to keep the offenders behind bars.

Underlying this program and many other effective nonprofit endeavors is a commitment to management. Twenty years ago, management was a dirty word for those involved in nonprofit organizations. It meant business, and nonprofits prided themselves on being free of the taint of commercialism and above such sordid considerations as the bottom line. Now most of them have learned that nonprofits need management even more than business does, precisely because they lack the discipline of the bottom line. The nonprofits are, of course, still dedicated to "doing good." But they also realize that good intentions are no substitute for organization and leadership, for accountability, performance, and results. Those require management and that, in turn, begins with the organization's mission.

As a rule, nonprofits are more money-conscious than business enterprises are. They talk and worry about money much of the time because it is so hard to raise and because they always have so much less of it than they need. But nonprofits do not base their strategy on money, nor do they make it the center of their plans, as so many corporate executives do. "The businesses I work with start their planning with financial returns," says one well-known CEO who sits on both business and nonprofit boards. "The nonprofits start with the performance of their mission."

Starting with the mission and its requirements may be the first lesson business can learn from successful nonprofits. It focuses the organization on action. It defines the specific strategies needed to attain the crucial goals. It creates a disciplined organization. It alone can prevent the most common degenerative disease of organizations, especially large ones: splintering their always limited resources on things that are "interesting" or look "profitable" rather than concentrating them on a very small number of productive efforts.

The best nonprofits devote a great deal of thought to defining their organization's mission. They avoid sweeping statements full of good intentions and focus, instead, on objectives that have clear-cut implications for the work their members perform – staff and volunteers both. The Salvation Army's goal, for example, is to turn society's rejects – alcoholics, criminals, derelicts – into citizens. The Girl Scouts

help youngsters become confident, capable young women who respect themselves and other people. The Nature Conservancy preserves the diversity of nature's fauna and flora. Nonprofits also start with the environment, the community, the "customers" to be; they do not, as American businesses tend to do, start with the inside, that is, with the organization or with financial returns.

Willowcreek Community Church in South Barrington, Illinois, outside Chicago, has become the nation's largest church – some 13,000 parishioners.

Nonprofits need management precisely because they don't have a bottom line.

Yet it is barely 15 years old. Bill Hybels, in his early twenties when he founded the church, chose the community because it had relatively few churchgoers, though the population was growing fast and churches were plentiful. He went from door to door asking, "Why don't you go to church?" Then he designed a church to answer the potential customers' needs: for instance, it offers full services on Wednesday evenings because many working parents need Sunday to spend with their children. Moreover, Hybels continues to listen and react. The pastor's sermon is taped while it is being delivered and instantly reproduced so that parishioners can pick up a cassette when they leave the building because he was told again and again, "I need to listen when I drive home or drive to work so that I can build the message into my life." But he was also told: "The sermon always tells me to change my life but never how to do it." So now every one of Hybels's sermons ends with specific action recommendations.

A well-defined mission serves as a constant reminder of the need to look outside the organization not only for "customers" but also for measures of success. The temptation to content oneself with the "goodness of our cause" – and thus to substitute good intentions for results – always exists in nonprofit organizations. It is precisely because of this that the successful and performing nonprofits have learned to define clearly what changes *outside* the organization constitute "results" and to focus on them.

The experience of one large Catholic hospital chain in the Southwest shows how productive a clear sense of mission and a focus on results can be. Despite the sharp cuts in Medicare payments and hospital stays during the past eight years, this chain has increased revenues by 15% (thereby managing to break even) while greatly expanding its services and raising both patient-care and medical standards. It has done so because the nun who is its CEO understood that she and her staff are in the business of delivering health care (especially to the poor), not running hospitals.

As a result, when health care delivery began moving out of hospitals for medical rather than economic reasons about ten years ago, the chain promoted the trend instead of fighting it. It founded ambulatory surgery centers, rehabilitation centers, X-ray and lab networks, HMOs, and so on. The chain's motto was: "If it's in the patient's interest, we have to promote it; it's then our job to make it pay." Paradoxically, the policy has filled the chain's hospitals; the freestanding facilities are so popular they generate a steady stream of referrals.

This is, of course, not so different from the marketing strategy of successful Japanese companies. But it is very different indeed from the way most Western businesses think and operate. And the difference is that the Catholic nuns—and the Japanese—start with the mission rather than with their own rewards, and with what they have to make happen outside themselves, in the marketplace, to deserve a reward.

Finally, a clearly defined mission will foster innovative ideas and help others understand why they need to be implemented—however much they fly in the face of tradition. To illustrate, consider the Daisy Scouts, a program for five-year-olds which the Girl Scouts initiated a few years back. For 75 years, first grade had been the minimum age for entry into a Brownie troop, and many Girl Scout councils wanted to keep it that way. Others, however, looked at demographics and saw the growing numbers of working women with "latch key" kids. They also looked at the children and realized that they were far more sophisticated than their predecessors a generation ago (largely thanks to TV).

Today the Daisy Scouts are 100,000 strong and growing fast. It is by far the most successful of the many programs for preschoolers that have been started these last 20 years, and far more successful than any of the very expensive government programs. Moreover, it is so far the only program that has seen these critical demographic changes and children's exposure to long hours of TV viewing as an opportunity.

Many nonprofits now have what is still the exception in business—a functioning board. They also have something even rarer: a CEO who is clearly accountable to the board and whose performance is reviewed annually by a board committee. And they have what is rarer still: a board whose performance is reviewed annually against preset performance objectives. Effective use of the board is thus a second area in which business can learn from the nonprofit sector.

In U.S. law, the board of directors is still considered the "managing" organ of the corporation. Manage-

What do a large Catholic hospital chain and successful Japanese companies have in common?

ment authors and scholars agree that strong boards are essential and have been writing to that effect for more than 20 years, beginning with Myles Mace's pioneering work.[1] Nevertheless, the top managements of our large companies have been whittling away at the directors' role, power, and independence for more than half a century. In every single business failure of a large company in the last few decades, the board was the last to realize that things were going wrong. To find a truly effective board, you are much better advised to look in the nonprofit sector than in our public corporations.

In part, this difference is a product of history. Traditionally, the board has run the shop in nonprofit organizations—or tried to. In fact, it is only because nonprofits have grown too big and complex to be run by part-time outsiders, meeting for three hours a month, that so many have shifted to professional management. The American Red Cross is probably the largest nongovernmental agency in the world and certainly one of the most complex. It is responsible for worldwide disaster relief; it runs thousands of blood banks as well as the bone and skin banks in hospitals; it conducts training in cardiac and respiratory rescue nationwide; and it gives first-aid courses in thousands of schools. Yet it did not have a paid chief executive until 1950, and its first professional CEO came only with the Reagan era.

But however common professional management becomes—and professional CEOs are now found in most nonprofits and all the bigger ones—nonprofit boards cannot, as a rule, be rendered impotent the way so many business boards have been. No matter how much nonprofit CEOs would welcome it—and quite a few surely would—nonprofit boards cannot become their rubber stamp. Money is one reason. Few directors in publicly held corporations are substantial shareholders, whereas directors on nonprofit boards very often contribute large sums themselves, and are expected to bring in donors as

1. A good example is Myles Mace, "The President and the Board of Directors," HBR March-April 1972, p. 37.

well. But also, nonprofit directors tend to have a personal commitment to the organization's cause. Few people sit on a church vestry or on a school board unless they deeply care about religion or education. Moreover, nonprofit board members typically have served as volunteers themselves for a good many years and are deeply knowledgeable about the organization, unlike outside directors in a business.

Precisely because the nonprofit board is so committed and active, its relationship with the CEO tends to be highly contentious and full of potential for friction. Nonprofit CEOs complain that their board "meddles." The directors, in turn, complain that management "usurps" the board's function. This has forced an increasing number of nonprofits to realize that neither board nor CEO is "the boss." They are colleagues, working for the same goal but

> ## The key to making a board effective is to organize its work, not talk about its function.

each having a different task. And they have learned that it is the CEO's responsibility to define the tasks of each, the board's and his or her own.

For example, a large electric co-op in the Pacific Northwest created ten board committees, one for every member. Each has a specific work assignment: community relations, electricity rates, personnel, service standards, and so on. Together with the co-op's volunteer chairman and its paid CEO, each of these one-person committees defines its one-year and three-year objectives and the work needed to attain them, which usually requires five to eight days a year from the board member. The chairman reviews each member's work and performance every year, and a member whose performance is found wanting two years in a row cannot stand for reelection. In addition, the chairman, together with three other board members, annually reviews the performance of the entire board and of the CEO.

The key to making a board effective, as this example suggests, is not to talk about its function but to organize its work. More and more nonprofits are doing just that, among them half a dozen fair-sized liberal arts colleges, a leading theological seminary, and some large research hospitals and museums. Ironically, these approaches reinvent the way the first nonprofit board in America was set up 300 years ago: the Harvard University Board of Overseers. Each member is assigned as a "visitor" to one area in the university—the Medical School, the Astronomy Department, the investment of the endowment—and

acts both as a source of knowledge to that area and as a critic of its performance. It is a common saying in American academia that Harvard has the only board that makes a difference.

The weakening of the large corporation's board would, many of us predicted (beginning with Myles Mace), weaken management rather than strengthen it. It would diffuse management's accountability for performance and results; and indeed, it is the rare big-company board that reviews the CEO's performance against preset business objectives. Weakening the board would also, we predicted, deprive top management of effective and credible support if it were attacked. These predictions have been borne out amply in the recent rash of hostile takeovers.

To restore management's ability to manage we will have to make boards effective again—and that should be considered a responsibility of the CEO. A few first steps have been taken. The audit committee in most companies now has a real rather than a make-believe job responsibility. A few companies—though so far almost no large ones—have a small board committee on succession and executive development, which regularly meets with senior executives to discuss their performance and their plans. But I know of no company so far where there are work plans for the board and any kind of review of the board's performance. And few do what the larger nonprofits now do routinely: put a new board member through systematic training.

Nonprofits used to say, "We don't pay volunteers so we cannot make demands upon them." Now they are more likely to say, "Volunteers must get far greater satisfaction from their accomplishments and make a greater contribution precisely because they do not get a paycheck." The steady transformation of the volunteer from well-meaning amateur to trained, professional, unpaid staff member is the most significant development in the nonprofit sector—as well as the one with the most far-reaching implications for tomorrow's businesses.

A Midwestern Catholic diocese may have come furthest in this process. It now has fewer than half the priests and nuns it had only 15 years ago. Yet it has greatly expanded its activities—in some cases, such as help for the homeless and for drug abusers, more than doubling them. It still has many traditional volunteers like the Altar Guild members who arrange flowers. But now it is also being served by some 2,000 part-time unpaid staff who run the Catholic charities, perform administrative jobs in parochial schools, and organize youth activities, college Newman Clubs, and even some retreats.

A similar change has taken place at the First Baptist Church in Richmond, Virginia, one of the largest and oldest churches in the Southern Baptist Convention. When Dr. Peter James Flamming took over five years ago, the church had been going downhill for many years, as is typical of old, inner-city churches. Today it again has 4,000 communicants and runs a dozen community outreach programs as well as a full complement of in-church ministries. The church has only nine paid full-time employees. But of its 4,000 communicants, 1,000 serve as unpaid staff.

This development is by no means confined to religious organizations. The American Heart Association has chapters in every city of any size throughout the country. Yet its paid staff is limited to those at national headquarters, with just a few traveling troubleshooters serving the field. Volunteers manage and staff the chapters, with full responsibility for community health education as well as fund raising.

These changes are, in part, a response to need. With close to half the adult population already serving as volunteers, their overall number is unlikely to grow. And with money always in short supply, the nonprofits cannot add paid staff. If they want to add to their activities – and needs are growing – they have to make volunteers more productive, have to give them more work and more responsibility. But the major impetus for the change in the volunteer's role has come from the volunteers themselves.

More and more volunteers are educated people in managerial or professional jobs – some preretirement men and women in their fifties, even more babyboomers who are reaching their mid-thirties or forties. These people are not satisfied with being help-

> Nonprofits used to say, "We don't pay volunteers so we can't demand much." Now they say, "Because we don't pay, we have to demand even more."

ers. They are knowledge workers in the jobs in which they earn their living, and they want to be knowledge workers in the jobs in which they contribute to society – that is, their volunteer work. If nonprofit organizations want to attract and hold them, they have to put their competence and knowledge to work. They have to offer meaningful achievement.

Many nonprofits systematically recruit for such people. Seasoned volunteers are assigned to scan the newcomers – the new member in a church or synagogue, the neighbor who collects for the Red Cross – to find those with leadership talent and persuade them to try themselves in more demanding assignments. Then senior staff (either a full-timer on the payroll or a seasoned volunteer) interviews the newcomers to assess their strengths and place them accordingly. Volunteers may also be assigned both a mentor and a supervisor with whom they work out their performance goals. These advisers are two different people, as a rule, and both, ordinarily, volunteers themselves.

The Girl Scouts, which employs 730,000 volunteers and only 6,000 paid staff for 3½ million girl members, works this way. A volunteer typically starts by driving youngsters once a week to a meeting. Then a more seasoned volunteer draws her into other work – accompanying Girl Scouts selling cookies door-to-door, assisting a Brownie leader on a camping trip. Out of this step-by-step process evolve the volunteer boards of the local councils and, eventually, the Girl Scouts governing organ, the National Board. Each step, even the very first, has its own compulsory training program, usually conducted by a woman who is herself a volunteer. Each has specific performance standards and performance goals.

What do these unpaid staff people themselves demand? What makes them stay – and, of course, they can leave at any time. Their first and most important demand is that the nonprofit have a clear mission, one that drives everything the organization does. A senior vice president in a large regional bank has two small children. Yet she just took over as chair of the state chapter of Nature Conservancy, which finds, buys, and manages endangered natural ecologies. "I love my job," she said, when I asked her why she took on such heavy additional work, "and of course the bank has a creed. But it doesn't really know what it contributes. At Nature Conservancy, I know what I am here for."

The second thing this new breed requires, indeed demands, is training, training, and more training. And, in turn, the most effective way to motivate and hold veterans is to recognize their expertise and use them to train newcomers. Then these knowledge workers demand responsibility – above all, for thinking through and setting their own performance goals. They expect to be consulted and to participate in making decisions that affect their work and the work of the organization as a whole. And they expect opportunities for advancement, that is, a chance to take on more demanding assignments and more responsibility as their performance warrants. That is why a good many nonprofits have developed career ladders for their volunteers.

Supporting all this activity is accountability. Many of today's knowledge-worker volunteers insist on having their performance reviewed against preset objectives at least once a year. And increasingly, they expect their organizations to remove nonperformers by moving them to other assignments that better fit their capacities or by counseling them to leave. "It's worse than the Marine Corps boot camp," says the priest in charge of volunteers in the Midwestern diocese, "but we have 400 people on the waiting list." One large and growing Midwestern art museum requires of its volunteers—board members, fundraisers, docents, and the people who edit the museum's newsletter—that they set their goals each year, appraise themselves against these goals each year, and resign when they fail to meet their goals two years in a row. So does a fair-sized Jewish organization working on college campuses.

These volunteer professionals are still a minority, but a significant one—perhaps a tenth of the total volunteer population. And they are growing in numbers and, more important, in their impact on the nonprofit sector. Increasingly, nonprofits say what the minister in a large pastoral church says: "There is no laity in this church; there are only pastors, a few paid, most unpaid."

This move from nonprofit volunteer to unpaid professional may be the most important development in American society today. We hear a great deal about the decay and dissolution of family and community and about the loss of values. And, of course, there is reason for concern. But the

> ## When I ask executives why they volunteer, too many say, "Because there isn't enough challenge in my job."

nonprofits are generating a powerful countercurrent. They are forging new bonds of community, a new commitment to active citizenship, to social responsibility, to values. And surely what the nonprofit contributes to the volunteer is as important as what the volunteer contributes to the nonprofit. Indeed, it may be fully as important as the service, whether religious, educational, or welfare related, that the nonprofit provides in the community.

This development also carries a clear lesson for business. Managing the knowledge worker for pro-

"You look like you mean business, Hadley."

ductivity is the challenge ahead for American management. The nonprofits are showing us how to do that. It requires a clear mission, careful placement and continuous learning and teaching, management by objectives and self-control, high demands but corresponding responsibility, and accountability for performance and results.

There is also, however, a clear warning to American business in this transformation of volunteer work. The students in the program for senior and middle-level executives in which I teach work in a wide diversity of businesses: banks and insurance companies, large retail chains, aerospace and computer companies, real estate developers, and many others. But most of them also serve as volunteers in nonprofits—in a church, on the board of the college they graduated from, as scout leaders, with the YMCA or the Community Chest or the local symphony orchestra. When I ask them why they do it, far too many give the same answer: Because in my job there isn't much challenge, not enough achievement, not enough responsibility; and there is no mission, there is only expediency.

Reprint 89404

Management and the World's Work

by Peter F. Drucker

When Marx was beginning work on *Das Kapital* in the early 1850s, the phenomenon of management was unknown. So were the enterprises that managers run. The largest manufacturing company around was a Manchester, England cotton mill employing fewer than 300 people, owned by Marx's friend and collaborator Friedrich Engels. And in Engels's mill—one of the most profitable businesses of its day — there were no "managers," only first-line supervisors, or charge hands, who were workers themselves, each enforcing discipline over a handful of fellow "proletarians."

Rarely in human history has any institution emerged as fast as management or had as great an impact as quickly. In less than 150 years, management has transformed the social and economic fabric of the world's developed countries. It has created a global economy and set new rules for countries that would participate in that economy as equals. And it has itself been transformed.

To be sure, the fundamental task of management remains the same: to make people capable of joint performance by giving them common goals, common values, the right structure, and the ongoing training and development they need to perform and to respond to change. But the very meaning of this task has changed, if only because the performance of management has converted the work force from one composed largely of unskilled laborers to one of highly educated knowledge workers.

Few executives are aware of the tremendous impact management has had. Indeed, a good many are like M. Jourdain, the character in Molière's *Le Bourgeois Gentilhomme*, who did not know that he spoke prose. They barely realize that they practice—or mispractice—management. As a result, they are ill-prepared for the tremendous challenges that come upon them. For the truly important problems

The truly important problems managers face come from the successes of management itself.

Peter F. Drucker, the Marie Rankin Clarke Professor of Social Sciences and Management at the Claremont Graduate School, is known throughout the world for his work on management practice and thought. This is his twenty-fifth article in HBR; the first appeared in 1950.

managers face do not come from technology or politics. They do not originate outside of management and enterprise. They are problems caused by the very success of management itself.

Eighty years ago, on the threshold of World War I, when a few people were just becoming aware of management's existence, most people in developed countries (perhaps four out of every five) earned their living in three occupations. There were domestic servants—in Great Britain, the largest single occupation (a full third of all workers), but a very large group everywhere, even in the United States. There were farmers—usually family farmers, who accounted for more than half the working population in every country except England and Belgium. And finally, there were blue-collar workers in manufacturing industries—the fastest growing occupation and the one that by 1925 would embrace almost 40% of the U.S. labor force.

Today domestic servants have all but disappeared. Full-time farmers account for only 3% to 5% of the working population in the non-Communist, developed countries, even though farm production is four to five times what it was 80 years ago. Blue-collar manufacturing employment is rapidly moving down the same path as farming. Manual workers employed in manufacturing in the United States now make up only 18% of the total work force; by the end of the century, they are likely to account for 10% or so in the United States and elsewhere—with manufacturing production steadily rising and expected to be at least 50% higher. The largest single group, more than one-third of the total, consists of workers whom the U.S. Bureau of the Census calls "managerial and professional." And a larger proportion of the total adult population than ever before—almost two-thirds in the United States, for instance—is now gainfully employed in every developed, non-Communist country.

Management has been the main agent of this unprecedented transformation. For it is management that explains why, for the first time in human history, we can employ large numbers of knowledgeable, skilled people in productive work. No earlier society could do this. Indeed, no earlier society could support more than a handful of such people because, until quite recently, no one knew how to put people with different skills and knowledge together to achieve common goals. Eighteenth century China was the envy of contemporary Western intellectuals because it supplied more jobs for educated people than all of Europe did—some 20,000 per year. Yet today, the United States with a roughly comparable population produces nearly one million college graduates a year, most of whom have little difficulty finding well-paid employment. What enables us to employ them is management.

Knowledge, especially advanced knowledge, is always highly specialized. By itself it produces nothing. Yet a modern large business can usefully employ up to 10,000 highly knowledgeable people who possess up to 60 different fields of knowledge. Engineers of all sorts, designers, marketing experts, economists, statisticians, psychologists, planners, accountants, human resources people—all work together in a joint venture, and none would be effective without the managed enterprise that is business.

The question of which came first—the educational explosion of the last 100 years or the management that could put this knowl-

For the first time in human history, we can employ large numbers of educated people productively.

edge to productive use – is moot. Modern management and modern enterprise clearly could not exist without the knowledge base that developed societies have built. But equally, it is management and management alone that makes all this knowledge and these knowledgeable people effective. The emergence of management has converted knowledge from a social ornament and luxury into what we now know to be the true capital of any economy.

And knowledge, in turn – instead of bricks and mortar – has become the center of capital investment. Japan invests a record 8% of its annual GNP in plant and equipment. But Japan invests at least twice as much in education, two-thirds in schools for the young, the rest in the training and teaching of adults (largely in the organizations that employ them). And the United States puts an even larger share – roughly 20% – of its much larger GNP into education and training. In the modern society of enterprise and management, knowledge is the primary resource and society's true wealth.

Not many business leaders could have predicted this development back in 1870, when large enterprises like those we know today were beginning to take shape. The reason was not so much lack of foresight as lack of precedent. At that time, the only large permanent organization around was the army. Not surprisingly, therefore, its command-and-control structure became the model for the men who were putting together transcontinental railroads, steel mills, modern banks, and department stores.

The command model, with a very few at the top giving orders and a great many at the bottom obeying them, remained the norm for nearly 100 years. But it was never as static as its longevity might suggest. On the contrary, it began to change almost at once, as specialized knowledge of all sorts poured into enterprise. The first university-trained engineer in manufacturing industry was hired in Germany in 1867, and within five years he had built a research department. Other specialties followed suit, and by World War I the familiar typical functions of a manufacturer had been developed: research and engineering, manufacturing, sales, finance and accounting, and a little later, human resources.

Even more important for its impact on enterprise – and on the world economy in general – was another management-directed development that took place at this time. That was the application of management to manual work in the form of training. The child of wartime necessity, training has propelled the transformation of the world economy in the last 30 years because it allows low-wage countries to do something that traditional economic theory had said could never be done: to become efficient – and yet still low-wage – competitors almost overnight.

Until World War I, it was axiomatic that it took a long time (Adam Smith said several hundred years) for a country or region to develop a tradition of labor and the expertise in manual and organizational skills needed to produce and market a given product, whether cotton textiles or violins. But during World War I, large numbers of totally unskilled, preindustrial people had to be made productive workers in practically no time. To meet this need, businesses in the United States and the United Kingdom began to apply Frederick Taylor's principles of "scientific management," developed between 1885 and 1910, to the systematic training of blue-collar workers on a large

Management has made knowledge the true capital of every economy.

Management substitutes systems and information for guesswork, toil, and brawn.

scale. They analyzed tasks and broke them down into individual, unskilled operations that could then be learned quite quickly. Further developed in World War II, training was then picked up by the Japanese and, 20 years later, by the South Koreans, who made it the basis for their countries' phenomenal development.

During the 1920s and 1930s, management was applied to many more areas and aspects of manufacturing business. Decentralization, for instance, arose to combine the advantages of bigness and the advantages of smallness within one enterprise. Accounting went from "bookkeeping" to analysis and control. Planning grew out of the "Gantt charts" designed in 1917 and 1918 to plan war production, and so did the use of analytical logic and statistics, which used quantification to convert experience and intuition into definitions, information, and diagnosis. Marketing similarly evolved as a result of applying management concepts to distribution and selling.

Moreover, as early as the mid-1920s and early 1930s, some management pioneers (Thomas Watson, Sr. at the fledgling IBM, General Robert E. Wood at Sears, Roebuck, and Elton Mayo at the Harvard Business School among them) began to question the way that manufacturing was organized. Eventually, they concluded that the assembly line was a short-term compromise despite its tremendous productivity: poor economics because of its inflexibility, poor use of human resources, even poor engineering. And so they began the thinking that eventually led to "automation" as the way to organize the manufacturing process, and to "Theory Y," teamwork, quality circles, and the information-based organization as the way to manage human resources.

Every one of these managerial innovations represented the application of knowledge to work, the substitution of system and information for guesswork, brawn, and toil. Every one, to use Frederick Taylor's terms, replaced "working harder" with "working smarter."

The powerful effect of these changes became apparent during World War II. To the very end, the Germans were by far the better strategists. And because they had the benefit of much shorter interior lines, they needed far fewer support troops and could match their opponents in combat strength. Yet the Allies won—their victory achieved by management.

The United States, with one-fifth the population, had almost as many men in uniform as all the other belligerents together. Yet it still produced more war material than all the others taken together. And it managed to get that material to fighting fronts as far apart as China, Russia, India, Africa, and Western Europe. No wonder, then, that by the war's end almost all the world had become management conscious. Or that management emerged as a recognizably distinct kind of work, one that could be studied and developed into a discipline—as happened in each of the countries that has exercised economic leadership during the postwar period.

But also, after World War II we began slowly to see that management is not *business* management. It pertains to every human effort that brings together in one organization people of diverse knowledge and skills. And it can be powerfully applied in hospitals, universities, churches, arts organizations, and social service agencies of all kinds. These "third sector" institutions have grown faster than either business or government in the developed countries since World

War II. And their leaders are becoming more and more management conscious. For even though the need to manage volunteers or raise funds may differentiate nonprofit managers from their for-profit peers, many more of their responsibilities are the same—among them, defining the right strategy and goals, developing people, measuring performance, and marketing the organization's services.

This is not to say that our knowledge of management is complete. Management education today is on the receiving end of a great deal of criticism, much of it justified. What we knew about management 40 years ago—and have codified in our systems of organized management education—does not necessarily help managers meet the challenges they face today. Nevertheless, that knowledge was the foundation for the spectacular expansion the world economy has undergone since 1950, in developed and developing countries alike. And what has made that knowledge obsolete is, in large measure, its own success in hastening the shift from manual work to knowledge work in business organizations.

To take just one example, we now have a great need for new accounting concepts and methods. Experts like Robert Kaplan, in his HBR article "Yesterday's Accounting Undermines Production" (July-August 1984), have pointed out that many of the assumptions on which our system is based are no longer valid. For example, accounting conventions assume that manufacturing industry is central; in fact, service and information industries are now more important in all developed countries. They also assume that a business produces just one product, whereas practically all modern businesses produce a great many different products. But above all, cost accounting, that proud invention of the mid-1920s, assumes that 80% of all costs are attributable to direct manual labor. In reality, manual labor in advanced manufacturing industries today accounts for no more than 8% to 12% of all costs. And the processes used in industries like automobiles and steel, in which labor costs are higher, are distinctly antiquated.

Efforts to devise accounting systems that will reflect changes like these—and provide accurate managerial information—are under way. But they are still in the early stages. So are our efforts to find solutions to other important management challenges: structures that work for information-based organizations; ways to raise the productivity of knowledge workers; techniques for managing existing businesses and developing new and very different ones at the same time; ways to build and manage truly global businesses; and many more.

Leadership in management—not technological innovation—made Japan a great economic power.

Management arose in developed countries. How does its rise affect the developing world? Perhaps the best way to answer this question is to start with the obvious: management and large enterprise, together with our new communications capacity, have created a truly global economy. In the process, they have changed what countries must do to participate effectively in that economy and to achieve economic success.

In the past, starring roles in the world's economy were always based on leadership in technological innovation. Great Britain became an economic power in the late eighteenth and early nineteenth centuries through innovation in the steam engine, machine tools, textiles, railroads, iron making, insurance, and international

*Development requires
a knowledge base
that few developing
countries possess
or can afford.*

banking. Germany's economic star rose in the second half of the nineteenth century on innovation in chemistry, electricity, electronics, optics, steel, and the invention of the modern bank. The United States emerged as an economic power at the same time through innovative leadership in steel, electricity, telecommunications, electronics, automobiles, agronomy, office equipment, agricultural implements, and aviation.

But the one great economic power to emerge in this century—Japan—has not been a technological pioneer in any area. Its ascendancy rests squarely on leadership in management. The Japanese understood the lessons of America's managerial achievement during World War II more clearly than we did ourselves—especially with respect to managing people as a resource rather than as a cost. As a result, they adapted the West's new "social technology"—management—to make it fit their own values and traditions. They adopted (and adapted) organization theory to become the most thorough practitioners of decentralization in the world. (Pre-World War II Japan had been completely centralized.) And they began to practice marketing when most American companies were still only preaching it.

Japan also understood sooner than other countries that management and technology together had changed the economic landscape. The mechanical model of organization and technology, which came into being at the end of the seventeenth century when an obscure French physicist, Denis Papin, designed a prototypical steam engine, came to an end in 1945, when the first atomic bomb exploded and the first computer went on line. Since then, the model for both technology and organizations has been a biological one—interdependent, knowledge intensive, and organized by the flow of information.

One consequence of this change is that the industries that have been the carriers of enterprise for the last 100 years—industries like automobiles, steel, consumer electronics, and appliances—are in crisis. And this is true even where demographics seem to be in their favor. For example, countries like Mexico and Brazil have an abundant supply of young people who can be trained easily for semi-skilled manual work. The mechanical industries would seem to be a perfect match. But as competitors in every industrial nation have found, mechanical production is antiquated unless it becomes automated—that is, unless it is restructured around information. For that reason alone, education is perhaps the greatest "management" challenge developing countries face.

Another way to arrive at the same conclusion is to look at a second fact with which developing countries must reckon: the developed countries no longer need them as they did during the nineteenth century. It may be hyperbole to say, as Japan's leading management consultant, Kenichi Ohmae, has said, that Japan, North America, and Western Europe can exist by themselves without the two-thirds of humanity who live in developing countries. But it is a fact that during the last 40 years the countries of this so-called triad have become essentially self-sufficient except for petroleum. They produce more food than they can consume—in glaring contrast to the nineteenth century. They produce something like three-fourths of all the world's manufactured goods and services. And they provide the market for an equal proportion.

This poses an acute problem for developing countries, even very big ones like China and India. They cannot hope to become important economic powers by tracking the evolution of enterprise and management—that is, by starting with nineteenth and early twentieth century industries and productive processes based mainly on a manual work force. Demographically they may have no choice, of course. And maybe they can even begin to catch up. But can they ever get ahead? I doubt it.

During the last 200 years, no country has become a major economic power by following in the footsteps of earlier leaders. Each started out with what were, at the time, advanced industries and advanced production and distribution processes. And each, very fast, became a leader in management. Today, however, in part because of automation information and advanced technology, but in much larger part because of the demand for trained people in all areas of management, development requires a knowledge base that few developing countries possess or can afford. How to create an adequate managerial knowledge base fast is the critical question in economic development today. It is also one for which we have no answer so far.

The problems and challenges discussed so far are largely internal to management and enterprise. But the most important challenge ahead for management in developed countries is the result of an external change that I first called "pension fund socialism" in my 1976 book, *The Unseen Revolution: How Pension Fund Socialism Came to America*. I am referring, of course, to the shift of the titles of ownership of public companies to the institutional trustees of the country's employees, chiefly through their pension funds.

Socially this is the most positive development of the twentieth century because it resolves the "Social Question" that vexed the nineteenth century—the conflict between "capital" and "labor"—by merging the two. But it has also created the most violent turbulence for management and managers since they arose a century ago. For pension funds are the ultimate cause of the explosion of hostile takeovers in the last few years; and nothing has so disturbed and demoralized managers as the hostile takeover. In this sense, takeovers are only a symptom of the fundamental questions pension fund socialism raises about the legitimacy of management: To whom are managers accountable? For what? What is the purpose and rationale of large, publicly owned enterprises?

In 1986, the last year for which we have figures, the pension funds of America's employees owned more than 40% of U.S. companies' equity capital and more than two-thirds of the equity capital of the 1,000 largest companies. The funds of large institutions (businesses, states, cities, public service and nonprofit institutions like universities, school districts, and hospitals) accounted for three-quarters of these holdings. The funds of individuals (employees of small businesses and the self-employed) accounted for the other fourth. (Mutual funds, which also represent the savings of wage earners rather than of "capitalists," hold another 5% to 10% of the country's equity capital.)

These figures mean that pension funds are already the primary suppliers of capital in the United States. Indeed, it is almost impossi-

Pension fund socialism resolves the age-old conflict between capital and labor.

Pension funds cause the hostile takeovers that demoralize managers and challenge the legitimacy of management.

ble to build a new business or expand an existing one unless pension-fund money is available. In the next few years, the funds' holdings will become even larger, if only because federal government employees now have a pension fund that invests in equity shares. Thus, by the year 2000, pension funds will hold at least two-thirds of the share capital of all U.S. businesses except the smallest. Through their pension funds, U.S. employees will be the true owners of the country's means of production.

The same development, with a lag of about ten years, is taking place in Great Britain, Japan, West Germany, and Sweden. It is also starting to appear in France, Italy, and the Netherlands.

This startling development was not foreseen, but it was inevitable—the result of several interdependent factors. First is the shift in income distribution that directs 90% or so of the GNP in non-Communist, developed countries into the wage fund. (The figure varies from 85% in the United States to 95% or more in the Netherlands and Denmark.) Indeed, economically the "rich" have become irrelevant in developed countries, however much they dominate the society pages and titillate TV viewers. Even the very rich have actually become much poorer in this century if their incomes are adjusted for inflation and taxation. To be in the same league as the "tycoon" of 1900, today's "super-rich" person would need a net worth of at least $50 billion—perhaps even $100 billion—and income to match. A few Arab oil sheiks may qualify, but surely no one in a developed country.

At the same time, wage earners' real incomes have risen dramatically. Few employees in turn-of-the-century America could lay aside anything beyond their mortgage payments or the premiums on funeral insurance. But since then, the American industrial worker's real income and purchasing power have grown more than 20 times larger, even though the number of hours worked has dropped by 50%. The same has occurred in all the other industrially developed countries. And it has happened fastest in Japan, where the real income of industrial workers may now be as much as 30 times what it was 80 years ago.

Demand for this income is essentially limitless because we are again in the midst of an intensively creative period. In the 60 years between 1856 and World War I, a technical or social innovation that led almost immediately to a new industry appeared, on average, once every 14 months. And this entrepreneurial explosion underlay the rise of the tycoons. We needed people like J.P. Morgan, John D. Rockefeller, Sr., Andrew Carnegie, Friedrich Krupp, and the Mitsui family who could finance whole industries out of their private pockets. Technical and social innovations are coming just as fast today. And the effect of all this energy is that companies and countries require enormous amounts of capital just to keep up, let alone move ahead—amounts that are several orders of magnitude larger than those the tycoons had to supply 80 years ago.

Indeed, the total pretax incomes of America's 1,000 highest income earners would be barely adequate to cover the capital needs of the country's private industry for more than three or four days. This holds true for all developed countries. In Japan, for instance, the pretax incomes of the country's 2,000 highest income earners just about equals what the country's private industry invests every two or three days.

These economic developments would have forced us in any event to make workers into "capitalists" and owners of productive resources. That pension funds became the vehicle—rather than mutual funds or direct individual investments in equity as everyone expected 30 years ago—is the result of the demographic shift that has raised life expectancies in developed countries from age 40 to the mid- and late-70s. The number of older people is much too large, and the years during which they need an income too many, for them to depend on support from their children. They must rely on monies they themselves have put aside during their earning years—and these funds have to be invested for long stretches of time.

That modern society requires an identity of interest between enterprise and employee was seen very early, not only by pre-Marxist socialists like Saint-Simon and Fourier in France and Robert Owen in Scotland but also by classical economists like Adam Smith and David Ricardo. Attempts to satisfy this need through worker ownership of business thus go back more than 150 years. Without exception, they have failed.

In the first place, worker ownership does not satisfy the workers' basic financial and economic needs. It puts all the workers' financial resources into the business that employs them. But the workers' needs are primarily long-term, particularly the need for retirement income many years hence. So to be a sound investment for its worker-owners, a business has to prosper for a very long time—and only one business out of every 40 or 50 ever does. Indeed, few even survive long enough. But worker ownership also *destroys* companies in the end because it always leads to inadequate capital formation, inadequate investment in research and development, and stubborn resistance to abandonment of outmoded, unproductive, and obsolete products, processes, plants, jobs, and work rules.

Zeiss Optical Works, the oldest worker-owned business around, lost its leadership position in consumer optics to the Americans and the Japanese for just this reason. Time and again, Zeiss's worker-owners preferred immediate satisfaction—higher wages, bonuses, benefits—to investing in research, new products, and new markets. Worker ownership underlies the near collapse of industry in contemporary Yugoslavia. And its shortcomings are so greatly hampering industry in China that the country's leaders are trying to shift to "contract management," which will expand managerial autonomy and check the power of "work councils" and worker-owners.

And yet, worker ownership of the means of production is not only a sound concept, it is also inevitable. Power follows property, says the old axiom. Both James Madison, in the *Federalist Papers*, and Karl Marx took it from the seventeenth century English philosopher, James Harrington, who in turn took it from Aristotle. It can be found in early Confucian writings as well. And since property has shifted to the wage earners in all developed countries, power has to follow. Yet unlike any other worker ownership of the means of production, pension fund socialism maintains the autonomy and accountability of enterprise and management, market freedom, competition, and the ability to change and to innovate.

But pension fund socialism does not function fully as yet. We can solve the financial and economic problems it presents. We know, for instance, that a pension fund must invest no more than a small frac-

Pension funds are owners legally obligated to be short-term investors...but business investments must be managed for the long run.

tion of its assets, 5% perhaps, in the shares of its own company or of any one company altogether. We know quite a bit, though not nearly enough, about how to invest pension fund money. But we still have to solve the basic sociopolitical problem: how to build the accomplished fact of employee ownership into the governance of both pension funds and businesses.

Pension funds are the legal owners of the companies in which they invest. But they not only have no "ownership interest"; as trustees for the ultimate beneficiaries, the employees, they also are legally obligated to be nothing but "investors," and short-term investors at that. That is why it is worker ownership that has made the hostile takeover possible. For as trustees, the pension funds must sell if someone bids more than the market price.

Whether hostile takeovers benefit shareholders is a hotly debated issue. That they have serious economic side effects is beyond question. The fear of a hostile takeover may not be the only reason American managements tend to subordinate everything—market standing, research, product development, service, quality, innovation—to the short term. But it is surely a major reason. Moreover, the hostile takeover is a frontal attack on management and managers. Indeed, what makes the mere threat of a takeover so demoralizing to managers (especially the middle managers and professionals on whom a business depends for its performance) is the raiders' barely concealed contempt, which management sees as contempt for wealth-producing work, and their work's subordination to financial manipulation.

For their part, the raiders and their financial backers maintain that management is solely accountable to the shareholders *whatever* their wishes, even if those represent nothing more than short-term speculative gains and asset stripping. This is indeed what the law says. But the law was written for early nineteenth century business conditions, well before large enterprise and management came into being. And while every free-market country has similar laws, not all countries hold to them. In Japan, for instance, custom dictates that larger companies exist mainly for the sake of their employees except in the event of bankruptcy; and Japanese economic performance and even Japanese shareholders have surely not suffered as a result. In West Germany too, large enterprises are seen as "going concerns," whose preservation is in the national interest and comes before shareholders' gains.

Both Japan and Germany have organized an extra-legal but highly effective way to hold business managements accountable, however, in the form of the voting control exercised by the big commercial banks of both countries. No such system exists in the United States (or the United Kingdom), nor could it possibly be constructed. And even in Japan and Germany, the hold of the banks is weakening fast.

So we must think through what management should be accountable for; and how and through whom its accountability can be discharged. The stockholders' interest, both short- and long-term, is one of the areas, to be sure. But it is only one.

One thing is clear to anyone with the slightest knowledge of political or economic history: the present-day assertion of "absolute shareholder sovereignty" (of which the boom in takeovers is the most spectacular manifestation) is the last hurrah of nineteenth

The boom in takeovers is the last hurrah of preindustrial capitalism.

century, basically preindustrial capitalism. It violates many people's sense of justice—as the upsurge of "populism" and anti-Wall Street rhetoric in the 1988 presidential campaign attest.

But even more important, no economy can perform if it puts what Thorstein Veblen, some 70 years ago, called "the acquisitive instinct" ahead of the "instinct of workmanship." Modern enterprise, especially large enterprise, can do its economic job—including making profits for the shareholders—only if it is being managed for the long run. Investments, whether in people, in products, in plants, in processing, in technology, or in markets, require several years of gestation before there is even a "baby," let alone full-grown results. Altogether far too much in society—jobs, careers, communities—depends on the economic fortunes of large enterprises to subordinate them completely to the interests of any one group, including shareholders.

How to make the interests of shareholders—and this means pension funds—compatible with the needs of the economy and society is thus the big issue pension fund socialism has to resolve. And it has to be done in a way that makes managements accountable, especially for economic and financial performance, and yet allows them to manage for the long term. How we answer this challenge will decide both the shape and place of management and the structure, if not the survival, of the free-market economy. It will also determine America's ability to compete in a world economy in which competitive long-range strategies are more and more the norm.

What managers do is the same all over the world. How they do it is embedded in their tradition and culture.

Finally, what is management? Is it a bag of techniques and tricks? A bundle of analytical tools like those taught in business schools? These are important, to be sure, just as the thermometer and a knowledge of anatomy are important to the physician. But what the evolution and history of management—its successes as well as its problems—teach is that management is, above all else, a very few, essential principles. To be specific:

1. Management is about human beings. Its task is to make people capable of joint performance, to make their strengths effective and their weaknesses irrelevant. This is what organization is all about, and it is the reason that management is the critical, determining factor. These days, practically all of us are employed by managed institutions, large and small, business and nonbusiness—and that is especially true for educated people. We depend on management for our livelihoods and our ability to contribute and achieve. Indeed, our ability to contribute to society at all usually depends as much on the management of the enterprises in which we work as it does on our own skills, dedication, and effort.

2. Because management deals with the integration of people in a common venture, it is deeply embedded in culture. What managers do in West Germany, in Britain, in the United States, in Japan, or in Brazil is exactly the same. How they do it may be quite different. Thus one of the basic challenges managers in a developing country face is to find and identify those parts of their own tradition, history, and culture that can be used as building blocks. The difference between Japan's economic success and India's relative backwardness, for instance, is largely explained by the fact that Japanese managers were able to plant imported management concepts in their own cultural soil and make them grow. Whether China's leaders can do the

same – or whether their great tradition will become an impediment to the country's development – remains to be seen.

3. Every enterprise requires simple, clear, and unifying objectives. Its mission has to be clear enough and big enough to provide a common vision. The goals that embody it have to be clear, public, and often reaffirmed. We hear a great deal of talk these days about the "culture" of an organization. But what we really mean by this is the commitment throughout an enterprise to some common objectives and common values. Without such commitment there is no enterprise; there is only a mob. Management's job is to think through, set, and exemplify those objectives, values, and goals.

4. It is also management's job to enable the enterprise and each of its members to grow and develop as needs and opportunities change. This means that every enterprise is a learning and teaching institution. Training and development must be built into it on all levels – training and development that never stop.

5. Every enterprise is composed of people with different skills and knowledge doing many different kinds of work. For that reason, it must be built on communication and on individual responsibility. Each member has to think through what he or she aims to accomplish – and make sure that associates know and understand that aim. Each has to think through what he or she owes to others – and make sure that others understand and approve. Each has to think through what is needed from others – and make sure that others know what is expected of them.

6. Neither the quantity of output nor the bottom line is by itself an adequate measure of the performance of management and enterprise. Market standing, innovation, productivity, development of people, quality, financial results – all are crucial to a company's performance and indeed to its survival. In this respect, an enterprise is like a human being. Just as we need a diversity of measures to assess the health and performance of a person, we need a diversity of measures for an enterprise. Performance has to be built into the enterprise and its management; it has to be measured – or at least judged – and it has to be continuously improved.

7. Finally, the single most important thing to remember about any enterprise is that there are no results inside its walls. The result of a business is a satisfied customer. The result of a hospital is a healed patient. The result of a school is a student who has learned something and puts it to work ten years later. Inside an enterprise, there are only cost centers. Results exist only on the outside.

About management, as about any other area of human work, much more could be said. Tools must be acquired and used. Techniques and any number of processes and procedures must be learned. But managers who truly understand the principles outlined above and truly manage themselves in their light will be achieving, accomplished managers – the kind of managers who build successful, productive, and achieving enterprises all over the world and who establish standards, set examples, and leave as a legacy both greater capacity to produce wealth and greater human vision.   ▽

Managers who understand the principles of management leave as a legacy greater capacity to produce wealth and greater human vision.

Reprint 88506

THE COMING OF THE NEW ORGANIZATION

by PETER F. DRUCKER

The typical large business 20 years hence will have fewer than half the levels of management of its counterpart today, and no more than a third the managers. In its structure, and in its management problems and concerns, it will bear little resemblance to the typical manufacturing company, circa 1950, which our textbooks still consider the norm. Instead it is far more likely to resemble organizations that neither the practicing manager nor the management scholar pays much attention to today: the hospital, the university, the symphony orchestra. For like them, the typical business will be knowledge-based, an organization composed largely of specialists who direct and discipline their own performance through organized feedback from colleagues, customers, and headquarters. For this reason, it will be what I call an information-based organization.

Businesses, especially large ones, have little choice but to become information-based. Demographics, for one, demands the shift. The center of gravity in employment is moving fast from manual and clerical workers to knowledge workers who resist the command-and-control model that business took from the military 100 years ago. Economics also dictates change, especially the need for large businesses to innovate and to be entrepreneurs. But above all, information technology demands the shift.

Advanced data-processing technology isn't necessary to create an information-based organization, of course. As we shall see, the British built just such an organization in India when "information technology" meant the quill pen, and barefoot runners were the "telecommunications" systems. But as advanced technology becomes more and more prevalent, we have to engage in analysis and

The large business 20 years hence is more likely to resemble a hospital or a symphony than a typical manufacturing company.

Peter F. Drucker is Marie Rankin Clarke Professor of Social Sciences and Management at the Claremont Graduate School, which recently named its management center after him. Widely known for his work on management practice and thought, he is the author of numerous articles and books, the most recent of which is The Frontiers of Management *(E.P. Dutton/Truman Talley Books, 1986). This is Mr. Drucker's twenty-fourth contribution to HBR.*

diagnosis – that is, in "information" – even more intensively or risk being swamped by the data we generate.

So far most computer users still use the new technology only to do faster what they have always done before, crunch conventional numbers. But as soon as a company takes the first tentative steps from data to information, its decision processes, management structure, and even the way its work gets done begin to be transformed. In fact, this is already happening, quite fast, in a number of companies throughout the world.

We can readily see the first step in this transformation process when we consider the impact of computer technology on capital-investment decisions. We have known for a long time that there is no one right way to analyze a proposed capital investment. To understand it we need at least six analyses: the expected rate of return; the payout period and the investment's expected productive life; the discounted present value of all returns through the productive lifetime of the investment; the risk in not making the investment or deferring it; the cost and risk in case of failure; and finally, the opportunity cost. Every accounting student is taught these concepts. But before the advent of data-processing capacity, the actual analyses would have taken many years of clerical toil to complete. Now anyone with a spreadsheet should be able to do them in a few hours.

The availability of this information transforms the capital-investment analysis from opinion into diagnosis, that is, into the rational weighing of alternative assumptions. Then the information transforms the capital-investment decision from an opportunistic, financial decision governed by the numbers into a business decision based on the probability of alternative strategic assumptions. So the decision both presupposes a business strategy and challenges that strategy and its assumptions. What was once a budget exercise becomes an analysis of policy.

Information transforms a budget exercise into an analysis of policy.

The second area that is affected when a company focuses its data-processing capacity on producing information is its organization structure. Almost immediately, it becomes clear that both the number of management levels and the number of managers can be sharply cut. The reason is straightforward: it turns out that whole layers of management neither make decisions nor lead. Instead, their main, if not their only, function is to serve as "relays" – human boosters for the faint, unfocused signals that pass for communication in the traditional pre-information organization.

One of America's largest defense contractors made this discovery when it asked what information its top corporate and operating managers needed to do their jobs. Where did it come from? What form was it in? How did it flow? The search for answers soon revealed that whole layers of management – perhaps as many as 6 out of a total of 14 – existed only because these questions had not been asked before. The company had had data galore. But it had always used its copious data for control rather than for information.

Information is data endowed with relevance and purpose. Converting data into information thus requires knowledge. And knowledge, by definition. is specialized. (In fact, truly knowledgeable people tend toward overspecialization, whatever their field, precisely because there is always so much more to know.)

The information-based organization requires far more specialists overall than the command-and-control companies we are accustomed to. Moreover, the specialists are found in operations, not at corporate headquarters. Indeed, the operating organization tends to become an organization of specialists of all kinds.

Information-based organizations need central operating work such as legal counsel, public relations, and labor relations as much as ever. But the need for service staffs—that is, for people without operating responsibilities who only advise, counsel, or coordinate— shrinks drastically. In its *central* management, the information-based organization needs few, if any, specialists.

Because of its flatter structure, the large, information-based organization will more closely resemble the businesses of a century ago than today's big companies. Back then, however, all the knowledge, such as it was, lay with the very top people. The rest were helpers or hands, who mostly did the same work and did as they were told. In the information-based organization, the knowledge will be primarily at the bottom, in the minds of the specialists who do different work and direct themselves. So today's typical organization in which knowledge tends to be concentrated in service staffs, perched rather insecurely between top management and the operating people, will likely be labeled a phase, an attempt to infuse knowledge from the top rather than obtain information from below.

Finally, a good deal of work will be done differently in the information-based organization. Traditional departments will serve as guardians of standards, as centers for training and the assignment of specialists; they won't be where the work gets done. That will happen largely in task-focused teams.

This change is already under way in what used to be the most clearly defined of all departments—research. In pharmaceuticals, in telecommunications, in papermaking, the traditional *sequence* of research, development, manufacturing, and marketing is being replaced by *synchrony*: specialists from all these functions work together as a team, from the inception of research to a product's establishment in the market.

How task forces will develop to tackle other business opportunities and problems remains to be seen. I suspect, however, that the need for a task force, its assignment, its composition, and its leadership will have to be decided on case by case. So the organization that will be developed will go beyond the matrix and may indeed be quite different from it. One thing is clear, though: it will require greater self-discipline and even greater emphasis on individual responsibility for relationships and for communications.

To say that information technology is transforming business enterprises is simple. What this transformation will require of companies and top managements is much harder to decipher. That is why I find it helpful to look for clues in other kinds of information-based organizations, such as the hospital, the symphony orchestra, and the British administration in India.

A fair-sized hospital of about 400 beds will have a staff of several hundred physicians and 1,200 to 1,500 paramedics divided among some 60 medical and paramedical specialities. Each specialty has its own knowledge, its own training, its own language. In each specialty, especially the paramedical ones like the clinical lab and physical

Traditional departments won't be where the work gets done.

therapy, there is a head person who is a working specialist rather than a full-time manager. The head of each specialty reports directly to the top, and there is little middle management. A good deal of the work is done in ad hoc teams as required by an individual patient's diagnosis and condition.

A large symphony orchestra is even more instructive, since for some works there may be a few hundred musicians on stage playing together. According to organization theory then, there should be several group vice president conductors and perhaps a half-dozen division VP conductors. But that's not how it works. There is only the conductor-CEO—and every one of the musicians plays directly to that person without an intermediary. And each is a high-grade specialist, indeed an artist.

But the best example of a large and successful information-based organization, and one without any middle management at all, is the British civil administration in India.[1]

The British ran the Indian subcontinent for 200 years, from the middle of the eighteenth century through World War II, without making any fundamental changes in organization structure or administrative policy. The Indian civil service never had more than 1,000 members to administer the vast and densely populated subcontinent—a tiny fraction (at most 1%) of the legions of Confucian mandarins and palace eunuchs employed next door to administer a not-much-more populous China. Most of the Britishers were quite young; a 30-year-old was a survivor, especially in the early years. Most lived alone in isolated outposts with the nearest countryman a day or two of travel away, and for the first hundred years there was no telegraph or railroad.

The organization structure was totally flat. Each district officer reported directly to the "Coo," the provincial political secretary. And since there were nine provinces, each political secretary had at least 100 people reporting directly to him, many times what the doctrine of the span of control would allow. Nevertheless, the system worked remarkably well, in large part because it was designed to ensure that each of its members had the information he needed to do his job.

Each month the district officer spent a whole day writing a full report to the political secretary in the provincial capital. He discussed each of his principal tasks—there were only four, each clearly delineated. He put down in detail what he had expected would happen with respect to each of them, what actually did happen, and why, if there was a discrepancy, the two differed. Then he wrote down what he expected would happen in the ensuing month with respect to each key task and what he was going to do about it, asked questions about policy, and commented on long-term opportunities, threats, and needs. In turn, the political secretary "minuted" every one of those reports—that is, he wrote back a full comment.

The best example of a large and successful information-based organization had no middle management at all.

---

1. The standard account is Philip Woodruff, *The Men Who Ruled India*, especially the first volume, *The Founders of Modern India* (New York: St. Martin's, 1954). How the system worked day by day is charmingly told in *Sowing* (New York: Harcourt Brace Jovanovich, 1962), volume one of the autobiography of Leonard Woolf (Virginia Woolf's husband).

On the basis of these examples, what can we say about the requirements of the information-based organization? And what are its management problems likely to be? Let's look first at the requirements. Several hundred musicians and their CEO, the conductor, can play together because they all have the same score. It tells both flutist and timpanist what to play and when. And it tells the conductor what to expect from each and when. Similarly, all the specialists in the hospital share a common mission: the care and cure of the sick. The diagnosis is their "score"; it dictates specific action for the X-ray lab, the dietitian, the physical therapist, and the rest of the medical team.

Information-based organizations, in other words, require clear, simple, common objectives that translate into particular actions. At the same time, however, as these examples indicate, information-based organizations also need concentration on one objective or, at most, on a few.

Because the "players" in an information-based organization are specialists, they cannot be told how to do their work. There are probably few orchestra conductors who could coax even one note out of a French horn, let alone show the horn player how to do it. But the conductor can focus the horn player's skill and knowledge on the musicians' joint performance. And this focus is what the leaders of an information-based business must be able to achieve.

Yet a business has no "score" to play by except the score it writes as it plays. And whereas neither a first-rate performance of a symphony nor a miserable one will change what the composer wrote, the performance of a business continually creates new and different scores against which its performance is assessed. So an information-based business must be structured around goals that clearly state management's performance expectations for the enterprise and for each part and specialist and around organized feedback that compares results with these performance expectations so that every member can exercise self-control.

The other requirement of an information-based organization is that everyone take information responsibility. The bassoonist in the orchestra does so every time she plays a note. Doctors and paramedics work with an elaborate system of reports and an information center, the nurse's station on the patient's floor. The district officer in India acted on this responsibility every time he filed a report.

The key to such a system is that everyone asks: Who in this organization depends on me for what information? And on whom, in turn, do I depend? Each person's list will always include superiors and subordinates. But the most important names on it will be those of colleagues, people with whom one's primary relationship is coordination. The relationship of the internist, the surgeon, and the anesthesiologist is one example. But the relationship of a biochemist, a pharmacologist, the medical director in charge of clinical testing, and a marketing specialist in a pharmaceutical company is no different. It, too, requires each party to take the fullest information responsibility.

Information responsibility to others is increasingly understood, especially in middle-sized companies. But information responsibility to oneself is still largely neglected. That is, everyone in an organization should constantly be thinking through what information he or she needs to do the job and to make a contribution.

Who depends on me for information? And on whom do I depend?

This may well be the most radical break with the way even the most highly computerized businesses are still being run today. There, people either assume the more data, the more information—which was a perfectly valid assumption yesterday when data were scarce, but leads to data overload and information blackout now that they are plentiful. Or they believe that information specialists know what data executives and professionals need in order to have information. But information specialists are tool makers. They can tell us what tool to use to hammer upholstery nails into a chair. We need to decide whether we should be upholstering a chair at all.

Executives and professional specialists need to think through what information is for them, what data they need: first, to know what they are doing; then, to be able to decide what they should be doing; and finally, to appraise how well they are doing. Until this happens MIS departments are likely to remain cost centers rather than become the result centers they could be.

Most large businesses have little in common with the examples we have been looking at. Yet to remain competitive—maybe even to survive—they will have to convert themselves into information-based organizations, and fairly quickly. They will have to change old habits and acquire new ones. And the more successful a company has been, the more difficult and painful this process is apt to be. It will threaten the jobs, status, and opportunities of a good many people in the organization, especially the long-serving, middle-aged people in middle management who tend to be the least mobile and to feel most secure in their work, their positions, their relationships, and their behavior.

The information-based organization will also pose its own special management problems. I see as particularly critical:

1. Developing rewards, recognition, and career opportunities for specialists.

2. Creating unified vision in an organization of specialists.

3. Devising the management structure for an organization of task forces.

4. Ensuring the supply, preparation, and testing of top management people.

To remain competitive—maybe even to survive—businesses will have to convert themselves into organizations of knowledgeable specialists.

Bassoonists presumably neither want nor expect to be anything but bassoonists. Their career opportunities consist of moving from second bassoon to first bassoon and perhaps of moving from a second-rank orchestra to a better, more prestigious one. Similarly, many medical technologists neither expect nor want to be anything but medical technologists. Their career opportunities consist of a fairly good chance of moving up to senior technician, and a very slim chance of becoming lab director. For those who make it to lab director, about 1 out of every 25 or 30 technicians, there is also the opportunity to move to a bigger, richer hospital. The district officer in India had practically no chance for professional growth except possibly to be relocated, after a three-year stint, to a bigger district.

Opportunities for specialists in an information-based business organization should be more plentiful than they are in an orchestra or hospital, let alone in the Indian civil service. But as in these organizations, they will primarily be opportunities for advancement within the specialty, and for limited advancement at that. Advancement into "management" will be the exception, for the simple reason that there will be far fewer middle-management positions to move into. This contrasts sharply with the traditional organization where, except in the research lab, the main line of advancement in rank is out of the specialty and into general management.

More than 30 years ago General Electric tackled this problem by creating "parallel opportunities" for "individual professional contributors." Many companies have followed this example. But professional specialists themselves have largely rejected it as a solution. To them—and to their management colleagues—the only meaningful opportunities are promotions into management. And the prevailing compensation structure in practically all businesses reinforces this attitude because it is heavily biased towards managerial positions and titles.

There are no easy answers to this problem. Some help may come from looking at large law and consulting firms, where even the most senior partners tend to be specialists, and associates who will not make partner are outplaced fairly early on. But whatever scheme is eventually developed will work only if the values and compensation structure of business are drastically changed.

The second challenge that management faces is giving its organization of specialists a common vision, a view of the whole.

In the Indian civil service, the district officer was expected to see the "whole" of his district. But to enable him to concentrate on it, the government services that arose one after the other in the nineteenth century (forestry, irrigation, the archaeological survey, public health and sanitation, roads) were organized outside the administrative structure, and had virtually no contact with the district officer. This meant that the district officer became increasingly isolated from the activities that often had the greatest impact on—and the greatest importance for—his district. In the end, only the provincial government or the central government in Delhi had a view of the "whole," and it was an increasingly abstract one at that.

A business simply cannot function this way. It needs a view of the whole and a focus on the whole to be shared among a great many of its professional specialists, certainly among the senior ones. And yet it will have to accept, indeed will have to foster, the pride and professionalism of its specialists—if only because, in the absence of opportunities to move into middle management, their motivation must come from that pride and professionalism.

One way to foster professionalism, of course, is through assignments to task forces. And the information-based business will use more and more smaller self-governing units, assigning them tasks tidy enough for "a good man to get his arms around," as the old phrase has it. But to what extent should information-based businesses rotate performing specialists out of their specialties and into new ones? And to what extent will top management have to accept as its top priority making and maintaining a common vision across professional specialties?

Heavy reliance on task-force teams assuages one problem. But it aggravates another: the management structure of the information-based organization. Who will the business's managers be? Will they be task-force leaders? Or will there be a two-headed monster—a specialist structure, comparable, perhaps, to the way attending physi-

Who will the business's managers be?

cians function in a hospital, and an administrative structure of task-force leaders?

The decisions we face on the role and function of the task-force leaders are risky and controversial. Is theirs a permanent assignment, analogous to the job of the supervisory nurse in the hospital? Or is it a function of the task that changes as the task does? Is it an assignment or a position? Does it carry any rank at all? And if it does, will the task-force leaders become in time what the product managers have been at Procter & Gamble: the basic units of management and the company's field officers? Might the task-force leaders eventually replace department heads and vice presidents?

Signs of every one of these developments exist, but there is neither a clear trend nor much understanding as to what each entails. Yet each would give rise to a different organizational structure from any we are familiar with.

With middle management sharply cut, where will the top executives come from?

Finally, the toughest problem will probably be to ensure the supply, preparation, and testing of top management people. This is, of course, an old and central dilemma as well as a major reason for the general acceptance of decentralization in large businesses in the last 40 years. But the existing business organization has a great many middle-management positions that are supposed to prepare and test a person. As a result, there are usually a good many people to choose from when filling a senior management slot. With the number of middle-management positions sharply cut, where will the information-based organization's top executives come from? What will be their preparation? How will they have been tested?

Decentralization into autonomous units will surely be even more critical than it is now. Perhaps we will even copy the German *Gruppe* in which the decentralized units are set up as separate companies with their own top managements. The Germans use this model precisely because of their tradition of promoting people in their specialties, especially in research and engineering; if they did not have available commands in near-independent subsidiaries to put people in, they would have little opportunity to train and test their most promising professionals. These subsidiaries are thus somewhat like the farm teams of a major-league baseball club.

We may also find that more and more top management jobs in big companies are filled by hiring people away from smaller companies. This is the way that major orchestras get their conductors—a young conductor earns his or her spurs in a small orchestra or opera house, only to be hired away by a larger one. And the heads of a good many large hospitals have had similar careers.

Can business follow the example of the orchestra and hospital where top management has become a separate career? Conductors and hospital administrators come out of courses in conducting or schools of hospital administration respectively. We see something of this sort in France, where large companies are often run by men who have spent their entire previous careers in government service. But in most countries this would be unacceptable to the organization (only France has the *mystique* of the *grandes écoles*). And even in France, businesses, especially large ones, are becoming too demanding to be run by people without firsthand experience and a proven success record.

Thus the entire top management process—preparation, testing, succession—will become even more problematic than it already is.

There will be a growing need for experienced businesspeople to go back to school. And business schools will surely need to work out what successful professional specialists must know to prepare themselves for high-level positions as *business* executives and *business* leaders.

Since modern business enterprise first arose, after the Civil War in the United States and the Franco-Prussian War in Europe, there have been two major evolutions in the concept and structure of organizations. The first took place in the ten years between 1895 and 1905. It distinguished management from ownership and established management as work and task in its own right. This happened first in Germany, when Georg Siemens, the founder and head of Germany's premier bank, *Deutsche Bank*, saved the electrical apparatus company his cousin Werner had founded after Werner's sons and heirs had mismanaged it into near collapse. By threatening to cut off the bank's loans, he forced his cousins to turn the company's management over to professionals. A little later, J.P. Morgan, Andrew Carnegie, and John D. Rockefeller, Sr. followed suit in their massive restructurings of U.S. railroads and industries.

The second evolutionary change took place 20 years later. The development of what we still see as the modern corporation began with Pierre S. du Pont's restructuring of his family company in the early twenties and continued with Alfred P. Sloan's redesign of General Motors a few years later. This introduced the command-and-control organization of today, with its emphasis on decentralization, central service staffs, personnel management, the whole apparatus of budgets and controls, and the important distinction between policy and operations. This stage culminated in the massive reorganization of General Electric in the early 1950s, an action that perfected the model most big businesses around the world (including Japanese organizations) still follow.[2]

Now we are entering a third period of change: the shift from the command-and-control organization, the organization of departments and divisions, to the information-based organization, the organization of knowledge specialists. We can perceive, though perhaps only dimly, what this organization will look like. We can identify some of its main characteristics and requirements. We can point to central problems of values, structure, and behavior. But the job of actually building the information-based organization is still ahead of us—it is the managerial challenge of the future. ▽

We can identify requirements and point to problems; the job of building is still ahead.

Reprint 88105

---

2. Alfred D. Chandler, Jr. has masterfully chronicled the process in his two books *Strategy and Structure* (Cambridge: MIT Press, 1962) and *The Visible Hand* (Cambridge: Harvard University Press, 1977)—surely the best studies of the administrative history of any major institution. The process itself and its results were presented and analyzed in two of my books: *The Concept of the Corporation* (New York: John Day, 1946) and *The Practice of Management* (New York: Harper Brothers, 1954).

Getting Things Done

Peter F. Drucker

How to make people decisions

There is no magic to good staffing and promotion decisions – just hard work and disciplined thought

Why is it that some managers have a golden touch when it comes to putting the right people in the right jobs? Have they mastered some abstruse method of predicting performance? Have they hit on some wondrous algorithm for personnel evaluation? Not at all, argues Peter Drucker, who draws on his long study of how effective managers operate to identify the key rules and assumptions for matching jobs with people. Instead of magic, what successful matching requires is careful understanding of the most important capabilities that a given job requires and of the strengths and weaknesses of each candidate. No mystery here, just good management.

Mr. Drucker is Clarke Professor of Social Sciences and Management at the Claremont Graduate School and professor emeritus of management at the Graduate Business School of New York University. He is the widely respected author of innumerable books and articles, including more than 20 contributions to HBR.

Executives spend more time on managing people and making people decisions than on anything else – and they should. No other decisions are so long lasting in their consequences or so difficult to unmake. And yet, by and large, executives make poor promotion and staffing decisions. By all accounts, their batting average is no better than .333: at most one-third of such decisions turn out right; one-third are minimally effective; and one-third are outright failures.

In no other area of management would we put up with such miserable performance. Indeed, we need not and should not. Managers making people decisions will never be perfect, of course, but they should come pretty close to batting 1,000 – especially since in no other area of management do we know as much.

Some executives' people decisions have, however, approached perfection. At the time of Pearl Harbor, every single general officer in the U.S. Army was overage. Although none of the younger men had been tested in combat or in a significant troup command, the United States came out of World War II with the largest corps of competent general officers any army has ever had. George C. Marshall, the army's chief of staff, had personally chosen each man. Not all were great successes, but practically none were outright failures.

In the 40 or so years during which he ran General Motors, Alfred P. Sloan, Jr. picked every GM executive – down to the manufacturing managers, controllers, engineering managers, and master mechanics at even the smallest accessory division. By today's standards, Sloan's vision and values may seem narrow. They were. He was concerned only with performance in and for GM. Nonetheless, his long-term performance in placing people in the right jobs was flawless.

The basic principles

There is no such thing as an infallible judge of people, at least not on this side of the Pearly Gates. There are, however, a few executives who take their people decisions seriously and work at them.

Marshall and Sloan were about as different as two human beings can be, but they followed, and quite consciously, much the same principles in making people decisions:

☐ If I put a person into a job and he or she does not perform, I have made a mistake. I have no business blaming that person, no business invoking the "Peter Principle," no business complaining. I have made a mistake.

☐ "The soldier has a right to competent command" was already an old maxim at the time of Julius Caesar. It is the duty of managers to make sure that the responsible people in their organizations perform.

☐ Of all the decisions an executive makes, none are as important as the decisions about people because they determine the performance capacity of the organization. Therefore, I'd better make these decisions well.

☐ The one "don't": do not give new people new major assignments, for doing so only compounds the risks. Give this sort of assignment to someone whose behavior and habits you know and who has earned trust and credibility within your organization. Put a high-level newcomer first into an established position where the expectations are known and help is available.

Some of the worst staffing failures I have seen involved brilliant Europeans hired by U.S. companies—one based in Pittsburgh; the other, Chicago—to head up new European ventures. Dr. Hans Schmidt and M. Jean Perrin (only the names are fictitious) were hailed as geniuses when they came in. A year later they were both out, totally defeated.

No one in Pittsburgh had understood that Schmidt's training and temperament would make him sit on a new assignment for the first six or nine months, thinking, studying, planning, getting ready for decisive action. Schmidt, in turn, had never even imagined that Pittsburgh expected instant action and immediate results. No one in Chicago had known that Perrin, while a solid and doggedly purposeful man, was excitable and mercurial, flailing his arms, making speeches about trivia, and sending up one trial balloon after another. Although both men subsequently became highly successful CEOs of major European corporations, both executives were failures in companies that did not know and understand them.

Two other U.S. companies successfully established businesses for the first time in Europe during the same period (the late 1960s and early 1970s). To initiate their projects, each sent to Europe a U.S. executive who had never before worked or lived there but whom people in the head offices knew thoroughly and understood well. In turn the two managers were thoroughly familiar with their companies. At the same time, each organization hired half a dozen young Europeans and placed them in upper-middle executive jobs in the United States. Within a few years, both companies had a solid European business and a trained, seasoned, and trusted corps of executives to run it.

As Winston Churchill's ancestor, the great Duke of Marlborough, observed some three centuries ago, "The basic trouble in coalition warfare is that one has to entrust victory if not one's life, to a fellow commander whom one knows by reputation rather than by performance."

In the corporation as in the military, without personal knowledge built up over a period of time there can be neither trust nor effective communication.

The decision steps

Just as there are only a few basic principles, there are only a few important steps to follow in making effective promotion and staffing decisions:

1   **Think through the assignment.** Job descriptions may last a long time. In one large manufacturing company, for example, the job description for the position of division general manager has hardly changed since the company began to decentralize 30 years ago. Indeed, the job description for bishops in the Roman Catholic church has not changed at all since canon law was first codified in the thirteenth century. But assignments change all the time, and unpredictably.

Once in the early 1940s, I told Alfred Sloan that he seemed to spend an inordinate amount of time pondering the assignment of a fairly low-level job—general sales manager of a small accessory division—before choosing among three equally qualified candidates. "Look at the assignment the last few times we had to fill the same job," Sloan answered. To my surprise, I found that the terms of the assignment were quite different on each occasion.

When putting a man in as division commander during World War II, George Marshall always looked first at the nature of the assignment for the next eighteen months or two years. To raise a division and train it is one assignment. To lead it in combat is quite another. To take command of a division that has been badly mauled and restore its morale and fighting strength is another still.

When the task is to select a new regional sales manager, the responsible executive must first know what the heart of the assignment is: to recruit and train new salespeople because, say, the present sales force is nearing retirement age? Or is it to open up new markets because the company's products, though doing well with old-line industries in the region, have not been able to penetrate new and growing markets? Or, since the bulk of sales still comes from products that are 25 years old, is it to establish a market presence for the company's new prod-ucts? Each of these is a different assignment and requires a different kind of person.

2   **Look at a number of potentially qualified people.** The controlling word here is "number." Formal qualifications are a minimum for consideration; their absence disqualifies the candidate automatically. Equally important, the person and the assignment need to fit each other. To make an effective decision, an executive should look at three to five qualified candidates.

3   **Think hard about how to look at these candidates.** If an executive has studied the assignment, he or she understands what a new person would need to do with high priority and concentrated effort. The central question is not "What can this or that candidate do or not do?" It is, rather, "What are the strengths each possesses and are these the right strengths for the assignment?" Weaknesses are limitations, which may, of course, rule a candidate out. For instance, a person may be excellently qualified for the technical aspects of a job; but if the assignment requires above all the ability to build a team and this ability is lacking, then the fit is not right.

But effective executives do not start out by looking at weaknesses. You cannot build performance on weaknesses. You can build only on strengths. Both Marshall and Sloan were highly demanding men, but both knew that what matters is the ability to do the assignment. If that exists, the company can always supply the rest. If it does not exist, the rest is useless.

If, for instance, a division needed an officer for a training assignment, Marshall looked for people who could turn recruits into soldiers. Every man that was good at this task usually had serious weaknesses in other areas. One was not particularly effective as a tactical commander and was positively hopeless when it came to strategy. Another had foot-in-mouth disease and got into trouble with the press. A third was vain, arrogant, egotistical, and fought constantly with his commanding officer. Never mind, could he train recruits? If the answer was yes—and especially if the answer was "he's the best"—he got the job.

In picking the members of their cabinets, Franklin Roosevelt and

Harry Truman said, in effect: "Never mind personal weaknesses. Tell me first what each of them can do." It may not be coincidence that these two presidents had the strongest cabinets in twentieth-century U.S. history.

4   **Discuss each of the candidates with several people who have worked with them.** One executive's judgment alone is worthless. Because all of us have first impressions, prejudices, likes, and dislikes, we need to listen to what other people think. When the military picks general officers or the Catholic church picks bishops, this kind of extensive discussion is a formal step in their selection process. Competent executives do it informally. Hermann Abs, the former head of Deutsche Bank, picked more successful chief executives in recent times than anyone else. He personally chose most of the top-level managers who pulled off the postwar German "economic miracle," and he checked out each of them first with three or four of the person's former bosses or colleagues.

5   **Make sure the appointee understands the job.** After the appointee has been in a new job for three or four months, he or she should be focusing on the demands of that job rather than on the requirements of preceeding assignments. It is the executive's responsibility to call that person in and say, "You have now been regional sales manager—or whatever—for three months. What do you have to do to be a success in your new job? Think it through and come back in a week or ten days and show me in writing. But I can tell you one thing right away: the things you did to get the promotion are almost certainly the wrong things to do now."

If you do not follow this step, don't blame the candidate for poor performance. Blame yourself. You have failed in your duty as a manager.

The largest single source of failed promotions—and I know of no greater waste in U.S. management—is the failure to think through, and help others think through, what a new job requires. All too typical is the brilliant former student of mine who telephoned me a few months ago, almost in tears. "I got my first big chance a year ago," he said. "My company made me engineering manager. Now they tell me that

I'm through. And yet I've done a better job than ever before. I have actually designed three successful new products for which we'll get patents."

It is only human to say to ourselves, "I must have done something right or I would not have gotten the big new job. Therefore, I had better do more of what I did to get the promotion now that I have it." It is not intuitively obvious to most people that a new and different job requires new and different behavior. Almost 50 years ago, a boss of mine challenged me four months after he had advanced me to a far more responsible position. Until he called me in, I had continued to do what I had done before. To his credit, he understood that it was his responsibility to make me see that a new job means different behavior, a different focus, and different relationships.

The high-risk decisions

Even if executives follow all these steps, some of their people decisions will still fail. These are, for the most part, the high-risk decisions that nevertheless have to be taken.

There is, for example, high risk in picking managers in professional organizations—for a research lab, say, or an engineering or corporate legal department. Professionals do not readily accept as their boss someone whose credentials in the field they do not respect. In choosing a manager of engineering, the choices are therefore limited to the top-flight engineers in the department. Yet there is no correlation (unless it be a negative one) between performance as a bench engineer and performance as a manager. Much the same is true when a high-performing operating manager gets a promotion to a staff job in headquarters or a staff expert moves into a line position. Temperamentally, operating people are frequently unsuited to the tensions, frustrations, and relationships of staff work, and vice versa. The first-rate regional sales manager may well become totally ineffective if promoted into market research, sales forecasting, or pricing.

We do not know how to test or predict whether a person's temperament will suit a new environment. We

can find this out only by experience. If a move from one kind of work to another does not pan out, the executive who made the decision has to remove the misfit, and fast. But that executive also has to say, "I made a mistake, and it is my job to correct it." To keep misfits in a job they cannot do is not being kind; it is being cruel. But there is also no reason to let the person go. A company can always use a good bench engineer, a good analyst, a good sales manager. The proper course of action—and it works most times—is to offer the misfit a return to the old job or an equivalent.

People decisions may also fail because a job has become what New England ship captains 150 years ago called a "widow maker." When a clipper ship, no matter how well designed and constructed, began to have fatal "accidents," the owners did not redesign or rebuild the ship. They broke it up as fast as possible.

Widow makers—that is, jobs that regularly defeat even good people—appear most often when a company grows or changes fast. For instance, in the 1960s and early 1970s, the job of "international vice president" in U.S. banks became a widow maker. It had always been an easy job to fill. In fact, it had long been considered a job in which banks could safely put "also rans" and could expect them to perform well. Then, suddenly, the job began to defeat one new incumbent after another. What had happened, as hindsight now tells us, is that international activity quickly and without warning became an integral part of the daily business of major banks and their corporate customers. What had been until then an easy job became, literally, a "nonjob" that nobody could do.

Whenever a job defeats two people in a row, who in their earlier assignments had performed well, a company has a widow maker on its hands. When this happens, a responsible executive should not ask the headhunter for a universal genius. Instead abolish the job. Any job that ordinarily competent people cannot perform is a job that cannot be staffed. Unless changed, it will predictably defeat the third incumbent the way it defeated the first two.

Making the right people decisions is the ultimate means of controlling an organization well. Such decisions reveal how competent management is, what its values are, and whether it takes its job seriously. No matter how hard managers try to keep their decisions a secret—and some still try hard—people decisions cannot be hidden. They are eminently visible.

Executives often cannot judge whether a strategic move is a wise one. Nor are they necessarily interested. "I don't know why we are buying this business in Australia, but it won't interfere with what we are doing here in Fort Worth" is a common reaction. But when the same executives read that "Joe Smith has been made controller in the XYZ division," they usually know Joe much better than top management does. These executives should be able to say, "Joe deserves the promotion; he is an excellent choice—just the person that division needs to get the controls appropriate for its rapid growth."

If, however, Joe got promoted because he is a politician, everybody will know it. They will all say to themselves, "Okay, that is the way to get ahead in this company." They will despise their management for forcing them to become politicians but will either quit or become politicians themselves in the end. As we have known for a long time, people in organizations tend to behave as they see others being rewarded. And when the rewards go to nonperformance, to flattery, or to mere cleverness, the organization will soon decline into nonperformance, flattery, or cleverness.

Executives who do not make the effort to get their people decisions right do more than risk poor performance. They risk losing their organization's respect. ▽

Reprint 85406

The discipline of innovation

Innovation can be systematically managed – if one knows where and how to look

Peter F. Drucker

As managers recognize the heightened importance of innovation to competitive success, they face an apparent paradox: the orderly and predictable decisions on which a business rests depend increasingly on the disorderly and unpredictable process of innovation. How can managers expect to plan for – or count on – a process that is itself so utterly dependent on creativity, inspiration, and old-fashioned luck? Drawing on his many years' experience studying innovative and entrepreneurial companies, the author argues that this paradox is apparent only, not real. Most of what happens in successful innovations is not the happy occurrence of a blinding flash of insight but, rather, the careful implementation of an unspectacular but systematic management discipline. At the heart of that discipline lies the knowledge of where to look for innovation opportunities and how to identify them. It is to this study of the sources of innovation that Mr. Drucker here addresses himself.

This article is adapted from chapters 2-11 of his new book, Innovation and Entrepreneurship: Practice and Principles, *published by Harper & Row. He is Clarke Professor of Social Science and Management at the Claremont Graduate School and professor emeritus of management at the Graduate Business School of New York University. He is also the widely respected author of numerous books and articles, including more than 20 contributions to HBR.*

Illustration by Gustav Szabo.

Despite much discussion these days of the "entrepreneurial personality," few of the entrepreneurs with whom I have worked during the last 30 years had such personalities. But I have known many people – salespeople, surgeons, journalists, scholars, even musicians – who did have them without being the least bit "entrepreneurial." What all the successful entrepreneurs I have met have in common is not a certain kind of personality but a commitment to the systematic practice of innovation.

Innovation is the specific function of entrepreneurship, whether in an existing business, a public service institution, or a new venture started by a lone individual in the family kitchen. It is the means by which the entrepreneur either creates new wealth-producing resources or endows existing resources with enhanced potential for creating wealth.

Today, much confusion exists about the proper definition of entrepreneurship. Some observers use the term to refer to all small businesses; others, to all new businesses. In practice, however, a great many well-established businesses engage in highly successful entrepreneurship. The term, then, refers not to an enterprise's size or age, but to a certain kind of activity. At the heart of that activity is innovation: the effort to create purposeful, focused change in an enterprise's economic or social potential.

Sources of innovation

There are, of course, innovations that spring from a flash of genius. Most innovations, however, especially the successful ones, result from a conscious, purposeful search for innovation opportunities, which are found only in a few situations.

Four such areas of opportunity exist *within* a company or industry:

Unexpected occurrences.

Incongruities.

Process needs.

Industry and market changes.

Three additional sources of opportunity exist *outside* a company in its social and intellectual environment:

Demographic changes.

Changes in perception.

New knowledge.

True, these sources overlap, different as they may be in the nature of their risk, difficulty, and complexity, and the potential for innovation may well lie in more than one area at a time. But among them, they account for the great majority of all innovation opportunities.

Unexpected occurrences

Consider, first, the easiest and simplest source of innovation opportunity: the unexpected. In the early 1930s, IBM developed the first modern accounting machine, which was designed for banks, but banks in 1933 did not buy new equipment. What saved the company—according to a story that Thomas Watson, Sr., the company's founder and long-term CEO, often told—was its exploitation of an unexpected success: the New York Public Library wanted to buy a machine. Unlike the banks, libraries in those early New Deal days had money, and Watson sold more than a hundred of his otherwise unsalable machines to libraries.

Fifteen years later, when everyone believed that computers were designed for advanced scientific work, business unexpectedly showed an interest in a machine that could do payroll. Univac, which had the most advanced machine, spurned business applications. But IBM immediately realized it faced a possible unexpected success, redesigned what was basically Univac's machine for such mundane applications as payroll, and within five years became the leader in the computer industry, a position it has maintained to this day.

The unexpected failure may be an equally important innovation opportunity source. Everyone

knows about the Ford Motor Company's Edsel as the biggest new car failure in automotive history. What very few people seem to know, however, is that the Edsel's failure was the foundation for much of the company's later success. Ford planned the Edsel, the most carefully designed car to that point in American automotive history, to give the company a full product line with which to compete with GM. When it bombed, despite all the planning, market research, and design that had gone into it, Ford realized that something was happening in the automobile market that ran counter to the basic assumptions on which GM and everyone else had been designing and marketing cars. No longer did the market segment primarily by income groups; suddenly, the new principle of segmentation was what we now call "life-styles." Ford's immediate responses were the Mustang and the Thunderbird—the cars that gave the company a distinct personality and reestablished it as an industry leader.

Unexpected successes and failures are such productive sources of innovation opportunities because most businesses dismiss them, disregard them, and even resent them. The German scientist who around 1906 synthesized novocaine, the first nonaddictive narcotic, had intended it to be used in major surgical procedures like amputation. Surgeons, however, preferred total anesthesia for such procedures; they still do. Instead, novocaine found a ready appeal among dentists. Its inventor spent the remaining years of his life traveling from dental school to dental school making speeches that forbade dentists to "misuse" his noble invention in applications for which he had not intended it.

This is a caricature, to be sure, but it illustrates the attitude managers often take to the unexpected: "It should not have happened." Corporate reporting systems further ingrain this reaction, for they draw attention away from unanticipated possibilities. The typical monthly or quarterly report has on its first page a list of problems, that is, the areas where results fall short of expectations. Such information is needed, of course; it helps prevent deterioration of performance.

But it also suppresses the recognition of new opportunities. The first acknowledgment of a possible opportunity usually applies to an area in which a company does better than budgeted. Thus genuinely entrepreneurial businesses have two "first pages"—a problem page and an opportunity page—and managers spend equal time on both.

Incongruities

Alcon Industries was one of the great success stories of the 1960s because Bill Connor, the

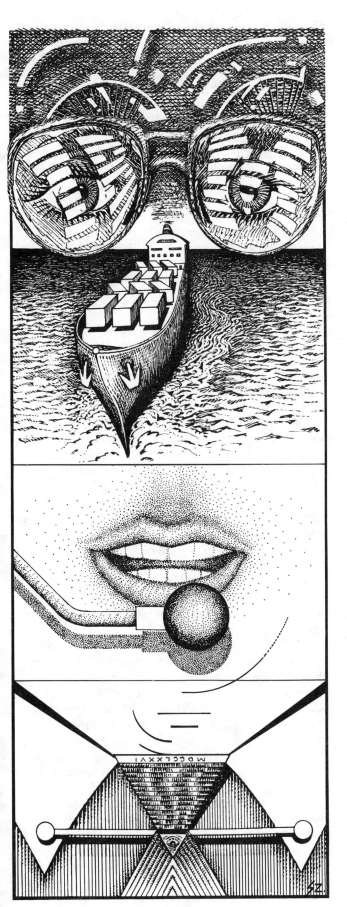

company's founder, exploited an incongruity in medical technology. The cataract operation is the world's third or fourth most common surgical procedure. During the last 300 years, doctors systematized it to the point that the only "old-fashioned" step left was the cutting of a ligament. Eye surgeons had learned to cut the ligament with complete success, but it was so different a procedure from the rest of the operation and so incompatible with it that they often dreaded it. It was incongruous.

Doctors had known for 50 years about an enzyme that could dissolve the ligament without cutting. All Connor did was to add a preservative to this enzyme that gave it a few months' shelf life. Eye surgeons immediately accepted the new compound, and Alcon found itself with a worldwide monopoly. Fifteen years later, Nestlé bought the company for a fancy price.

Such an incongruity within the logic or rhythm of a process is only one possibility out of which innovation opportunities may arise. Another source is incongruity between economic realities. For instance, whenever an industry has a steadily growing market but falling profit margins—as, say, in the steel industries of developed countries between 1950 and 1970—an incongruity exists. The innovative response: minimills.

An incongruity between expectations and results can also open up possibilities for innovation. For 50 years after the turn of the century, shipbuilders and shipping companies worked hard both to make ships faster and to lower their fuel consumption. Even so, the more successful they were in boosting speed and trimming fuel needs, the worse ocean freighter's economics became. By 1950 or so, the ocean freighter was dying, if not already dead.

All that was wrong, however, was an incongruity between the industry's assumptions and its realities. The real costs did not come from doing work (that is, being at sea) but from not doing work (that is, sitting idle in port). Once managers understood where costs truly lay, the innovations were obvious: the roll-on and roll-off ship and the container ship. These solutions, which involved old technology, simply applied to the ocean freighter what railroads and truckers had been using for 30 years. A shift in viewpoint, not in technology, totally changed the economics of ocean shipping and turned it into one of the major growth industries of the last 20 to 30 years.

Process needs

Anyone who has ever driven in Japan knows that the country has no modern highway system. Its roads still follow the paths laid down for—or by–oxcarts in the tenth century. What makes the system work for automobiles and trucks is an adaptation of the reflector used on American highways since the early 1930s. This reflector shows each car, which other cars are approaching, from any one of a half-dozen directions. This minor invention, which enables traffic to move smoothly and with a minimum of accidents, exploited a process need.

Around 1909, a statistician at the American Telephone & Telegraph Company projected two curves 15 years out: telephone traffic and American population. Viewed together, they showed that by 1920 or so every single female in the United States would have to work as a switchboard operator. The process need was obvious, and within two years, AT&T had developed and installed the automatic switchboard.

What we now call "media" also had their origin in two process need-based innovations around 1890. One was Mergenthaler's Linotype, which made it possible to produce a newspaper quickly and in large volume; the other was a social innovation, modern advertising, invented by the first true newspaper publishers, Adolph Ochs of the *New York Times,* Joseph Pulitzer of the *New York World,* and William Randolph Hearst. Advertising made it possible for them to distribute news practically free of charge, with the profit coming from marketing.

Industry & market changes

Managers may believe that industry structures are ordained by the Good Lord, but they can–and often do–change overnight. Such change creates tremendous opportunity for innovation.

One of American business's great success stories in recent decades is the brokerage firm of Donaldson, Lufkin & Jenrette, recently acquired by the Equitable Life Assurance Society. DL&J was founded in 1961 by three young men, all graduates of the Harvard Business School, who realized that the structure of the financial industry was changing as institutional investors became dominant. These young men had practically no capital and no connections. Still, within a few years, their firm had become a leader in the move to negotiated commissions and one of Wall Street's stellar performers. It was the first to be incorporated and go public.

In a similar fashion, changes in industry structure have created massive innovation opportunities for American health care providers. During the last 10 or 15 years, independent surgical and psychiatric clinics, emergency centers, and HMOs have opened throughout the country. Comparable opportunities in telecommunications followed industry upheavals– both in equipment (with the emergence of such companies as ROLM in the manufacturing of private branch exchanges) and in transmission (with the emergence of MCI and Sprint in long-distance service).

When an industry grows quickly–the critical figure seems to be in the neighborhood of a 40% growth rate over ten years or less–its structure changes. Established companies, concentrating on defending what they already have, tend not to counterattack when a newcomer challenges them. Indeed, when market or industry structures change, traditional industry leaders again and again neglect the fastest growing market segments. New opportunities rarely fit the way the industry has always approached the market, defined it, or organized to serve it. Innovators therefore have a good chance of being left alone for a long time.

Demographic changes

Of the outside sources of innovation opportunity, demographics are the most reliable. Demographic events have known lead times; for instance, every person who will be in the American labor force by the year 2000 has already been born. Yet, because policymakers often neglect demographics, those who watch them and exploit them can reap great rewards.

The Japanese are ahead in robotics because they paid attention to demographics. Everyone in the developed countries around 1970 or so knew that there was both a baby bust and an education explosion going on; half or more of the young people were now staying in school beyond high school. Consequently, the number of people available for traditional blue-collar work in manufacturing was bound to decrease and become inadequate by 1990. Everyone knew this, but only the Japanese acted on it and they now have a ten-year lead in robotics.

Much the same is true of Club Mediterranee's success in the travel and resort business. By 1970, thoughtful observers could have seen the emergence of large numbers of affluent and educated young adults in Europe and the United States. Not comfortable with the kind of vacations their working-class parents had enjoyed–the summer weeks at Brighton or Atlantic City–these young people were ideal customers for a new and exotic version of the "hangout" of their teen years.

Managers have known for a long time that demographics matter, but they have always believed that population statistics change slowly. In this century, however, they don't. Indeed, the innovation opportunities that changes in the numbers of people, and their age distribution, education, occupations, and geographic location make possible are among the most rewarding and least risky of entrepreneurial pursuits.

Changes in perception

"The glass is half-full" and "the glass is half-empty" are descriptions of the same phenomenon but have vastly different meanings. Changing a manager's perception of a glass from half-full to half-empty opens up big innovation opportunities.

All factual evidence indicates, for instance, that in the last 20 years, Americans' health has improved at unprecedented speed – whether measured by mortality rates for the newborn, survival rates for the very old, the incidence of cancers (other than lung cancer), cancer cure rates, or other factors. Even so, collective hypochondria grips the nation. Never before has there been so much concern with health or so much fear about health. Suddenly everything seems to cause cancer or degenerative heart disease or premature loss of memory. The glass is clearly half-empty.

Rather than rejoicing in great improvements in health, Americans seem to be emphasizing how far away they still are from immortality. This view of things has created many opportunities for innovations: markets for new health care magazines, for all kinds of health foods, and for exercise classes and jogging equipment. The fastest growing new U.S. business in 1983 was a company that makes indoor exercise equipment.

A change in perception does not alter facts. It changes their meaning, though – and very quickly. It took less than two years for the computer to change from being perceived as a threat and as something only big businesses would use to something one buys for doing income tax. Economics do not necessarily dictate such a change; in fact, they may be irrelevant. What determines whether people see a glass as half-full or half-empty is mood rather than fact, and change in mood often defies quantification. But it is not exotic or intangible. It is concrete. It can be defined. It can be tested. And it can be exploited for innovation opportunity.

New knowledge

Among history-making innovations, those based on new knowledge – whether scientific, technical, or social – rank high. They are the superstars of entrepreneurship; they get the publicity and the money. They are what people usually mean when they talk of innovation, though not all innovations based on knowledge are important. Some are trivial.

Knowledge-based innovations differ from all others in the time they take, in their casualty rates, and in their predictability, as well as in the challenges they pose to entrepreneurs. Like most superstars, they can be temperamental, capricious, and hard to direct. They have, for instance, the longest lead time of all innovations. There is a protracted span between the emergence of new knowledge and its distillation into usable technology. Then, there is another long period before this new technology appears in the marketplace in products, processes, or services. Overall, the lead time involved is something like 50 years, a figure that has not shortened appreciably throughout history.

To become effective, innovation of this sort usually demands not one kind of knowledge but many. Consider one of the most potent knowledge-based innovations: modern banking. The theory of the entrepreneurial bank – that is, of the purposeful use of capital to generate economic development – was formulated by the Comte de Saint-Simon during the era of Napoleon. Despite Saint-Simon's extraordinary prominence, it was not until 30 years after his death in 1826 that two of his disciples, the brothers Jacob and Isaac Pereire, established the first entrepreneurial bank, the Crédit Mobilier, and ushered in what we now call "finance capitalism."

The Pereires, however, did not know modern commercial banking, which developed at about the same time across the channel in England. The Crédit Mobilier failed ignominiously. Ten years later, two young men – one an American, J.P. Morgan, and one a German, Georg Siemens – put together the French theory of entrepreneurial banking and the English theory of commercial banking to create the first successful modern banks, J.P. Morgan & Company in New York and the Deutsche Bank in Berlin. Another ten years later, a young Japanese, Shibusawa Eiichi, adopted Siemens' concept to his country and thereby laid the foundation of Japan's modern economy. This is how knowledge-based innovation always works.

The computer, to cite another example, required no fewer than six separate strands of knowledge:

Binary arithmetic; Charles Babbage's conception of a calculating machine in the first half of the nineteenth century; the punch card, invented by Herman Hollerith for the U.S. census of 1890; the audion tube, an electronic switch invented in 1906; symbolic logic, which was created between 1910 and 1913 by Bertrand Russell and Alfred North Whitehead; and the concepts of programming and feedback that came out of abortive attempts during World War I to develop effective anti-aircraft guns. Although all the necessary knowledge was available by 1918, the first operational computer did not appear until 1946.

Long lead times and the need for convergence among different kinds of knowledge explain the peculiar rhythm of knowledge-based innovation, its attractions, and its dangers. During a long gestation period, there is a lot of talk and little action. Then, when all the elements suddenly converge, there is tremendous excitement and activity and an enormous amount of speculation. Between 1880 and 1890, for example, almost 1,000 electrical apparatus companies were founded in developed countries. Then, as always, there was a crash and a shakeout. By 1914, only 25 of these companies were still alive. In the early 1920s, 300 to 500 automobile companies existed in the United States; by 1960, only 4 remained.

It may be difficult, but knowledge-based innovation can be managed. Success requires careful analysis of the various kinds of knowledge needed to make an innovation possible. Both J.P. Morgan and Georg Siemens did this when they established their banking ventures. The Wright brothers did this when they developed the first operational airplane.

Careful analysis of the needs and, above all, the capabilities of the intended user is also essential. It may seem paradoxical, but knowledge-based innovation is more market dependent than any other kind of innovation.

De Havilland, a British company, designed and built the first passenger jet airplane, but it did not analyze what the market needed and therefore did not identify two key factors. One was configuration—that is, the right size with the right payload for the routes on which a jet would give an airline the greatest advantage. The other was equally mundane: how the airlines could finance the purchase of such an expensive plane. Because De Havilland failed to do an adequate user analysis, two American companies, Boeing and Douglas, took over the commercial jet aircraft industry.

Principles of innovation

Purposeful, systematic innovation begins with the analysis of the sources of new opportunities. Depending on the context, sources will have different importance at different times. Demographics, for instance, may be of little concern to innovators in fundamental industrial processes like steel making, although Mergenthaler's Linotype machine became successful primarily because there were not enough skilled typesetters available to satisfy a mass market. By the same token, new knowledge may be of little relevance to someone innovating a social instrument to satisfy a need that changing demographics or tax laws have created. But—whatever the situation—innovators must analyze all opportunity sources.

Because innovation is both conceptual and perceptual, would-be innovators must also go out and look, ask, and listen. Successful innovators use both the right and left sides of their brains. They look at figures. They look at people. They work out analytically what the innovation has to be to satisfy an opportunity. Then they go out and look at potential users to study their expectations, their values, and their needs.

To be effective, an innovation has to be simple and it has to be focused. It should do only one thing; otherwise it confuses people. Indeed, the greatest praise an innovation can receive is for people to say: "This is obvious! Why didn't I think of it? It's so simple!" Even the innovation that creates new users and new markets should be directed toward a specific, clear, and carefully designed application.

Effective innovations start small. They are not grandiose. They try to do one specific thing. It may be to enable a moving vehicle to draw electric power while it runs along rails, the innovation that made possible the electric streetcar. Or it may be the elementary idea of putting the same number of matches into a matchbox (it used to be 50). This simple notion made possible the automatic filling of matchboxes and gave the Swedes a world monopoly on matches for half a century. By contrast, grandiose ideas for things that will "revolutionize an industry" are unlikely to work.

In fact, no one can foretell whether a given innovation will end up a big business or a modest achievement. But even if the results are modest, the successful innovation aims from the beginning to become the standard setter, to determine the direction of a new technology or a new industry, to create the business that is—and remains—ahead of the pack. If an innovation does not aim at leadership from the beginning, it is unlikely to be innovative enough.

Above all, innovation is work rather than genius. It requires knowledge. It often requires ingenuity. And it requires focus. There are clearly people who are more talented as innovators than others but their talents lie in well-defined areas. Indeed, innovators rarely work in more than one area. For all his systematic innovative accomplishments, Edison worked only in the electrical field. An innovator in financial areas, Citibank for example, is not likely to embark on innovations in health care.

In innovation as in any other endeavor, there is talent, there is ingenuity, and there is knowledge. But when all is said and done, what innovation requires is hard, focused, purposeful work. If diligence, persistence, and commitment are lacking, talent, ingenuity, and knowledge are of no avail.

There is, of course, far more to entrepreneurship than systematic innovation: distinct entrepreneurial strategies, for example, and the principles of entrepreneurial management, which are needed equally in the established enterprise, the public service organization, and the new venture. But the very foundation of entrepreneurship—as a practice and as a discipline—is the practice of systematic innovation. ▽

Reprint 85307

*From the front lines
of economic activity
comes an unexpected bit of
happy news:
Americans are at last
learning how to manage
entrepreneurship*

Our entrepreneurial economy

Peter F. Drucker

Wrenching structural changes in the nation's industrial base have largely obscured an important new reality: small, new businesses have formed the main driving force for the nation's economic growth. More important, these businesses are by no means limited to high-tech industries. In field after field, especially in the service sector, technological advances, demographic shifts, and the availability of capital have encouraged start-up ventures to challenge conventional wisdom and experiment with new approaches to the market. Out of his broad familiarity with historical patterns of business development, the author sees this burst of entrepreneurial activity to be distinctive in its systematic application of good management practice.

Mr. Drucker is Clarke Professor of Social Science and Management at the Claremont Graduate School and professor emeritus of management at the Graduate Business School of New York University. He is the widely respected author of numerous books and articles, including more than 20 contributions to HBR, and has for many years studied, written about, and consulted with entrepreneurial companies.

Illustrations by Robert Pryor.

It is no longer news that small and new businesses provided most of the 20-odd million new jobs generated from 1970 to 1980 by the American economy. What is not generally known, however, is that this trend has continued, has even accelerated, during the recent recession. Indeed, over the last three years, *Fortune* "500" companies have lost some three million jobs, but businesses less than ten years old have *added* at least 750,000 jobs and slightly more than a million new employees.

This trend is almost the exact opposite of the typical post-World War II pattern. Between 1950 and 1970, either big businesses or governments created three out of every four new domestic jobs. In any downturn, job losses centered in new and small enterprises. From 1950 to 1970, then, the growth dynamics of the American economy lay in established institutions, but since 1970–and especially since 1979–these dynamics have moved to the entrepreneurial sector.

Life after high tech

Contrary to "what everybody knows," high-tech activities–that is, computers, gene splicing, and so on–account for only a small portion of this entrepreneurial sector. True, of the *Inc.* "100" (the 100 fastest growing, publicly owned companies that are not less than 5 or more than 15 years old), one-quarter are computer-related. But the *Inc.* sample consists of publicly owned new companies and is hardly representative of the whole entrepreneurial group: it has a quite heavy bias in the direction of high tech. Even so, last year there were five restaurant chains in the group, two women's wear manufacturers, and several health care providers.

High-tech companies get more than their share of attention because they are fashionable and fairly easy to finance through public stock offerings. By contrast, such equally fast growing operations as leasing companies, specialized hand tool makers, barbershop chains, and providers of continuing education are far less glamorous and so, far less in the public eye. Somewhat more visible are the transportation services like Federal Express and Emery Air Freight, whose success has forced our stodgiest bureaucracy, the U.S. Post Office, into inaugurating Express Mail— its first real innovation since it was pushed, kicking and screaming, into parcel post all of 70 years ago.

Altogether, a good deal less than one-third of the new entrepreneurship is in high tech. The rest divides fairly evenly into what people usually mean when they say "services" (restaurants, money market funds, and the like) and so-called primary activities that create wealth-producing capacity (education and training, health care, and information). Nor is this flurry of entrepreneurship confined to the Sunbelt. To be sure, 20 of the *Inc.* "100" are in California, but the same number are in the supposedly stagnant Mid-Atlantic region: New York, New Jersey, and Pennsylvania. Minnesota has 7, Colorado 5.

Remember, too, that the *Inc.* "100" and similar lists contain only businesses, although the new entrepreneurship is by no means confined to businesses. It is going strong in what we are beginning to call the "Third Sector"—nonprofit but nongovernmental activities. While the government conducts one study after another of the crises in health care, the Third Sector is busily creating new health care institutions—some founded by hospitals, some in competition with them, but each designed to turn the crisis into an entrepreneurial opportunity. There are, for example, independent clinics for diagnosis and primary care; ambulatory surgical centers; centers for psychiatric diagnosis and treatment; and freestanding maternity "motels."

Public schools may be closing, but entrepreneurship flourishes in private nonprofit education. In the suburban area in which I live, a neighborhood baby-sitting cooperative, founded by a few mothers some six years ago, has grown into a school with 200 children. A "Christian" school established a few years ago by the local Baptists is taking over from the city of Claremont a 15-year-old junior high school, which has stood vacant for lack of pupils for the last five years. Continuing education of all kinds— executive management programs for mid-career managers and refresher courses for doctors, engineers, lawyers, and physical therapists—is growing again after a temporary setback in 1981 and 1982.

The most important area of entrepreneurship, however, may well be an emerging "Fourth Sector" of public-private partnerships, in which governmental units, usually municipalities, determine performance standards and contract out for services— like fire protection, garbage collection, and bus transportation—to private companies on the basis of competitive bids. The city of Lincoln, Nebraska has since 1975 pioneered in efforts to couple better service with lower costs. This is, of course, the same Lincoln, Nebraska where the Populists and William Jennings Bryan first led the way toward municipal ownership of public services a hundred years ago. In Minneapolis, Control Data Corporation is building innovative public-private partnerships in education and even in the management and rehabilitation of prisoners.

The entrepreneurial surge is not entirely confined to the United States. Britain now has a booming Unlisted Securities Market (comparable to our over-the-counter market), which allows young and growing companies to raise capital without the great expense of a stock market underwriting. In Japan the fastest growing company during the last ten years has not been a transistor maker or an automobile company but a retail chain that acquired licenses from the United States for 7-Eleven food stores and Denny's restaurants. Italy, too, has a thriving entrepreneurial sector, but it is largely part of the "gray" economy and so does not appear in the figures of tax collectors or government statisticians. In France, however, the Mitterrand government has snuffed out much entrepreneurial activity by its move toward centralized planning and government control of credit.

On balance, however, the wave of entrepreneurial activity is primarily an American phenomenon. With respect to the steel, automobile, and consumer electronics industries, America shares equally in the crisis that afflicts all developed countries, Japan included. But in entrepreneurship—in creating the different and the new—the United States is way out in front.

The sources of entrepreneurialism

By any reasonable measure, then, the entrepreneurial economy in America is a fact. But how can we explain its emergence? Four major developments suggest themselves:

1   The rapid evolution of knowledge and technology made it possible, even 15 years ago, to see that the last decades of the twentieth century would more closely resemble the last decades of the nineteenth (when a new major technology leading almost at once to the emergence of a new industry appeared

on average every 18 months) than they would the 50 years following World War I. And we can say with high confidence that we are no more than midway into this period of renewed technology-based entrepreneurship.

Within the next 15 years, for example, we will surely see the most profound changes in the way we teach and learn since the printed book was introduced 500 years ago. The computer has, of course, a highly visible part to play here, but the real agent for educational change is the new scientific knowledge we have gained since Wilhelm Wundt in Germany and William James in this country first asked, 100 years ago, "How do we learn?"

2   Demographic trends explain a good deal of what is happening in service industries. The rapid growth of restaurant chains is a response to the emergence of the two-earner family; entrepreneurial ventures in the continuing education of adults reflect the post-World War II emergence of very large numbers of well-schooled adults. Indeed, recent entrepreneurial ventures based primarily on demographics have proven more successful than those based on new scientific technologies.

3   During the last 15 years, the United States has developed a unique and fairly effective system for supplying venture capital. No longer must small businesses suffer from a lack of access to capital. Today, in fact, there may well be more venture capital available than ventures deserving investment.

This system, by and large, supplies financing only to enterprises that are well past their babyhood, have a good track record, and are capable of absorbing fairly large sums—say, $250,000 and up. But who nurtures the true start-up enterprise? And how? We really do not know, yet the money clearly is there. Nothing like this invisible, private, unorganized but effective funding mechanism existed 20 or 30 years ago. Even though the published figures on capital formation and investment give no clue, what must have happened—apparently only in the United States—is a massive shift of individual investors toward private, local start-up ventures.

4   Finally, and perhaps most important, American industry has begun to learn how to manage entrepreneurship. Even established companies like IBM have done remarkably well as entrepreneurs, as have several of the larger pharmaceutical companies and financial institutions. The vigor shown these past few years by our largest and most traditionbound private business, AT&T, is surely worthy of note. More extraordinary still is the entrepreneurial spirit and competence of the one industry that everyone, 30 years ago, had given up for dead—the American railroad.

One railroad company, CSX, which grew out of the merger of the old Chesapeake & Ohio with the equally old Atlantic Coast Line, is now integrating railroads, barge lines, pipelines, slurry lines, and trucking lines into the world's first total land-transportation system. Another railroad, the Southern, has single-handedly changed transportation pricing and rate-making. A third, Union Pacific, is leading in developing the natural resources along its lines and in its territory.

Developing managerial skill

Many of the new entrepreneurs have learned what almost none of their predecessors knew: why and how to manage. Indeed, the very businesses they are in often involve the application of systematic management.

In the past, for example, barbershops were rarely profitable; at most they provided a working-class wage to a few people, including the owner, who was a working barber himself. Not one of these shops could have afforded a paid "manager," nor were there any chains of shops under common ownership. Today, however, one of the fastest growing and most profitable new ventures is a chain of barbershops in the Southwest, in which each unit is run by a manager earning an above-average middle-class salary.

Neither of the two young men who conceived, designed, and now manage the chain had worked in a barbershop before. What they did was ask the simple question, "What are the key elements in the performance of a barbershop?" The answer: store location; full utilization of barbers and barber chairs (that is, minimum "downtime"); standardized, high-quality work done at scheduled times; and no waiting on the part of customers.

Accordingly, they studied the location of successful barbershops and found that what everybody in the trade "knew" was wrong. They also discovered that 30-second spots on local TV were their most effective selling tool. This discovery led to their decision to open simultaneously ten or more shops in one metropolitan area—a decision that enabled them to go immediately on local TV and to break even within three months instead of the customary three years. Finally, they developed a three-month training program for managers, applied routine time-and-motion analysis to barbering, standardized the seemingly endless diversity of hairstyles and haircuts, and reduced the time needed for a good haircut by almost 60%. They were, as a result, able to eliminate waiting time.

Indeed, their ads say, "If you don't sit in a barber chair within twelve and a half minutes after you enter our shop, your haircut is on us."

Consider, too, a quite different type of fast-growing chain in the Midwest: psychiatric centers. This venture grew out of an analysis of the demands on a psychiatric-psychological practice. To the surprise of the chain's founder, it turned out that the segmentation of demands, their frequency, their seriousness, and the resources needed to meet them were predictable within margins of plus or minus 7.5%.

By constructing a diagnostic profile for the initial examination, the founders made it possible for a paramedic, usually a social worker with little or no formal psychiatric training, to do new patients' workups and determine the appropriate referral: to a psychiatrist, to a clinical psychologist, to a family counselor, to a social worker, or whatever. The profile also helps identify the few true exceptions when a senior professional should examine a new patient immediately. A group of seniors, one of whom has actually seen each patient, then reviews these conclusions once a week.

The whole process represents an MBO program of textbook purity: each staff member, patient, and patient category (e.g., alcoholics) has objectives for both diagnosis and treatment, which are reviewed against actual results every three months. A follow-up service, headed up by a woman whose former experience was as a dealer-service representative for one of the major Japanese automobile companies, keeps in contact with former patients on a systematic schedule.

Birth of a profession

What these and other new "service" entrepreneurs are doing is to apply to their businesses the analysis that Frederick Taylor first applied 100 years ago to the tasks of manual workers and that Georges Doriot of the Harvard Business School applied 50 years ago to manufacturing. These systematic management practices also distinguish today's successful high-tech entrepreneurs. Entrepreneurs of an earlier generation neither had nor wanted to acquire the weight of accumulated knowledge on managing people, communications, team formation, marketing, cash flow, and even innovation itself.

The new entrepreneurs, however, tend to have management training and attend management seminars and programs in massive numbers. Many—maybe most—become entrepreneurs only after they develop managerial experience in large organizations. Indeed, management students—even those at the prestigious business schools—increasingly see entrepreneurship as their ultimate aim and as the career for which their education best prepares them. Although it has become fashionable to contrast a supposedly obsolete "managerial" era of the past with a triumphantly emerging "entrepreneurial" era, it makes better sense to see in this flowering of an entrepreneurial economy the triumph of systematic management.

But also, clearly something important has happened to fairly large numbers of young Americans—to their attitudes, their values, their aspirations. Where are all the "hedonists," the "status seekers," the "me-tooers," and the "conformists" of the recent past? They are not turning out as David Riesman in *The Lonely Crowd,* or William H. Whyte in *The Organization Man,* or even Charles Reich in *The Greening of America* predicted. Without doubt, the emergence of the entrepreneurial economy is as much a cultural and psychological, as it is an economic or technological, event.

Implications for policy

These developments argue quite strongly that most "scientific" diagnoses of the nation's present economic ills are highly suspect. We are, for example, very likely *not* to be, as Jay W. Forrester and his group at MIT claim we are, in a long-term Kondratieff trough, but in the first stages of a long-term Kondratieff expansion.[1]

The Russian Nikolai Kondratieff, one of the founders of mathematical economics, 60 years ago identified a 50-year business cycle based on the inherent logic of technology. Typically, in the last decades of one of these cycles, old and mature industries seem to do exceptionally well, earning record profits and providing record employment. Actually, they are already in decline, for what looks like record profits is in fact underinvestment and the distribution of no-longer-needed capital.

When fast decline becomes manifest, there follows a 20-year trough, a long period of stagnation, low profits, and unemployment. Although the next generation of technologies may already exist, those technologies do not yet absorb enough capital or generate enough employment to fuel the economic growth needed to initiate another period of expansion.

There is, however, an atypical Kondratieff cycle. Industries based on old and mature technol-

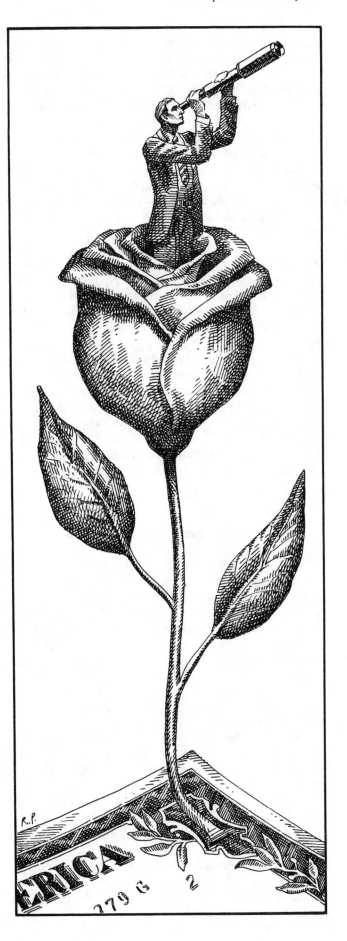

1 For an example, see Jay W. Forrester, "A Longer View of Current Economic Conditions," Systems Dynamic Group

Working Paper No. D-3405 (Cambridge: MIT, Sloan School Of Management, March 24, 1983).

ogies do indeed quickly decline, as is the case today in all developed countries. But industries based on new technologies and market opportunities grow so rapidly that they generate the requisite investment demand and employment to produce overall economic growth. As Joseph Schumpeter and others have shown, the Kondratieff trough experienced by Great Britain and France in the late nineteenth century simply did not happen in the United States or Germany. True, old and mature industries did decline; overall, however, there was rapid economic growth, not stagnation. Industries based on new technologies and market opportunities grew fast enough to provide investment demand and employment.

The surest indication of such an atypical cycle—and precisely what we see about us today in the United States—is the emergence of entrepreneurs across a spectrum of activities that extends far beyond what at the time is considered high tech. It is, to be sure, a period of high risk, rapid change, considerable turbulence, and severe anxiety. Real dangers abound that have nothing to do with business cycles—the threat of war, for example, or of the collapse of raw material producers. Nevertheless, it is a period of great opportunity, of fast-growing employment in certain areas, and of rapid overall growth. And as Schumpeter understood, what distinguishes such an atypical cycle from a more conventional trough is not the play of abstract economic forces. It is entrepreneurial energy.

What role for government?

As another national election approaches, discussion grows ever more heated about what government should do during this time of industrial transition. One line of argument, best represented by Robert Reich's *The Next American Frontier*, presses for government *not* to support employment in the old smokestack industries but to hasten their automation while subsidizing their redundant blue-collar workers. The key assumption here—that we will more quickly regain industrial leadership the sooner we decrease blue-collar manual employment in traditional mass-production industries—has good historical precedent. During the past 40 years, the faster we reduced blue-collar manual employment on the land, the more regularly we boosted agricultural production.

Reich's advice to his fellow Democrats that they put more distance between themselves and their traditional base of support among blue-collar unions, though novel, is surely shrewd and well taken. But his complementary suggestion to call on big government for central planning of the new high technologies—even if good politics—is wretched economics and bound to fail.

This questionable suggestion assumes that high tech is by itself where most future economic growth will happen. It clearly is not. It comprises only a part of the arena for growth, and by no means the main part. The biggest areas with the largest high-paying employment opportunities are elsewhere: in health care, for instance, and in continuing education. Government planning centered on high-tech industries will inevitably miss major growth areas.

Furthermore, can government really plan for the unknown? Whether planning is done Russian-style, Japanese-style, or French-style, it aims, by definition, at "catching up"—that is, at doing what some other country has already done but doing it better, more quickly, and with fewer mistakes, false starts, and failures. Hence, efforts to plan for the unknown have always ended up, like French high-tech planning under Mitterrand in the last three years, in misallocation of resources, frustration, and bad guesses about true growth areas. No one can plan for what does not yet exist; all one can do is encourage or discourage it.

How then do we encourage entrepreneurial growth in the American economy? Of course, we must guard against sacrificing tomorrow on the altar of yesterday, as the British have done so consistently for the past 30 years. Of course, we must cushion the impact of falling employment in the old smokestack industries. Doing all this without hurting the capacity of new employers to generate new jobs is going to be excruciatingly difficult and will require political decisions as hard as any ever made in this country.

Beyond trying not to stunt this new economic growth, the only thing government can effectively do is to remove obstacles. Indeed, the greatest help government can provide the entrepreneurial economy is to assuage the most crippling ailment of infant enterprises: their chronic cash shortage. Exempting new enterprises for five to seven years from taxes on profits retained in the business would not cost the Treasury much. But it might well be the most effective industrial policy of all. ▽

Reprint 84105

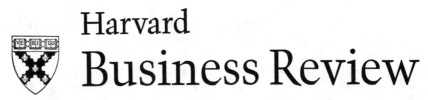

Harvard
Business Review

Peter F. Drucker

New templates
for today's organizations

*Traditional structures are no longer adequate
for today's complex organizations;
new designs are required to serve their needs*

Today's businesses are increasingly complex and diverse. In this article, a well-known organization theorist describes new principles of organization design now in use and their applications to today's businesses and institutions. It is his position that not only must the new principles make it possible for organizations to function and perform, but they must also serve the higher goals of human endeavor.

Mr. Drucker has contributed many articles to HBR and has authored several books, including *The Effective Executive* and *The Practice of Management*. The present article is a consolidation of several chapters from his new book, *Management: Tasks, Responsibilities, Practices*, published this year by Harper & Row. Until 1972, Mr. Drucker was professor of management at New York University. He is now Clarke Professor of Social Science at Claremont Graduate School, Claremont, California.

Organization structures are becoming increasingly short-lived and unstable.

The "classical" organization structures of the 1920s and 1930s, which still serve as textbook examples, stood for decades without needing more than an occasional touching up. American Telephone & Telegraph, General Motors, Du-Pont, Unilever, and Sears, Roebuck maintained their organizational concepts, structures, and basic components through several management generations and major changes in the size and scope of the business. Today, however, a company no sooner finishes a major job of reorganizing itself than it starts all over again.

General Electric, for instance, finished a tremendous organization overhaul around 1960, after almost a decade of hard work; since then it has revamped both its structure and its overall strategies at least twice. Similarly, Imperial Chemicals in Great Britain is restructuring an organization design that is barely 10 years old. And the same restlessness and instability afflict organization structures and concepts in the large U.S. commercial banks, in IBM, and in U.S. government agencies. For instance, the Health, Education and Welfare Department has been subjected to a "final" reorganization almost every year in its 20-year history.

To some extent this instability is a result of gross overorganizing. Companies are resorting to reorganization as a kind of miracle drug in lieu of diagnosing their ailments. Every business observer can see dozens of cases where substantial, even massive organization surgery is being misapplied to take care of a fairly minor procedural problem, or—even more often—to avoid facing up to personnel decisions. Equally common is the misuse of reorganization as a substitute for hard thinking on objectives, strategies, and priorities. Few managers seem to recognize that the right organization structure is not performance itself, but rather a prerequisite of performance. The wrong structure is indeed a guarantee of nonperformance; it produces friction and frustration, puts the spotlight on the wrong issues, and makes mountains out of trivia. But "perfect organization" is like "perfect health": the test is the ills it does not have and therefore does not have to cure.

Even if unnecessary organization surgery were not as rampant in our institutions as unnecessary appendectomies, hysterectomies, and tonsillectomies are said to be in our hospitals, there would still be an organization crisis. Twenty years ago many managers had yet to learn that organization design and organization structure deserve attention, thinking, and hard work. Almost everyone accepts this today; indeed, organization studies have been one of the true "growth industries" of the past twenty years. But while a few years ago organization theory had "the answers," today all is confusion.

The crisis is simultaneously a crisis of organization theory and of organization practice. Ironically, what is happening is not at all what organization theorists like Chris Argyris, Warren Bennis, Douglas McGregor (and I myself) have been predicting for at least 10 years: pressures for a more free-form and humanistic organization that provides greater scope for personal fulfillment play almost no part in the present organization crisis. Instead the main causes of instability are *changes in the objective task*, in the kind of business and institution to be organized. This is at the root of the crisis of organization practice.

The organization theorists' traditional answer to "organization crisis"—more organization development—is largely irrelevant to this new problem. Sometimes they seem to be pushing old remedies to cure a disease that no one has heard of before, and that inhabits a totally unfamiliar type of body. The kind of business and institution to be organized today is an enormously different beast from that of 20 years ago.

These changes in the objective task have generated new design principles that do not fit traditional organization concepts. And therein lies the crisis of theory. On the other hand, the past 20 years have also seen the emergence of new understandings of which organization needs require the most attention, and of how to go about the job of analyzing organization needs and designing organization structures. Only when we have an idea of what the new "body" looks like can we begin to treat its ills.

In what follows I compare old models with new realities and describe the new design principles. These principles can be matched to the tasks of modern management as well as to the formal needs of all organizations, independent of their purpose. In exploring these relationships, we can discern a way to avoid the organization crisis that affects so many businesses and institutions.

The early models

Twice in the short history of management we have had the "final answer" to organization problems.

The first time was around 1910 when Henri Fayol, the French industrialist, thought through what were, to him, the universally valid functions of a manufacturing company. (I am using the word "function" in the common, management sense, not in the way Fayol used it to describe administrative concerns.) Of course, at that time the manufacturing business presented the one truly important organization problem.

Then in the early 1920s Alfred P. Sloan, Jr., in organizing General Motors, took the next step. He found "the answer" for organizing a

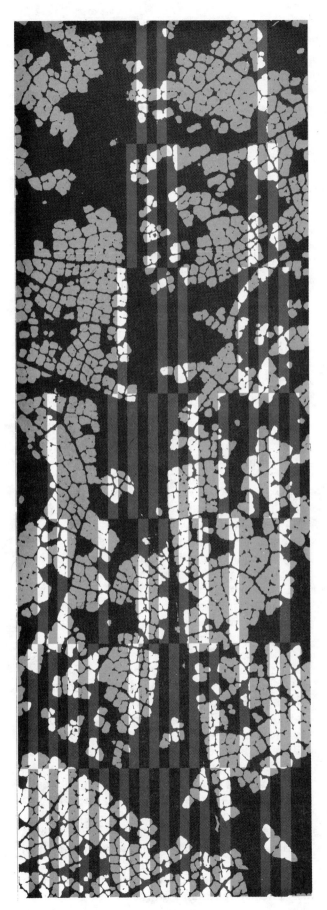

large, multidivisional manufacturing company. The Sloan approach built the individual divisions on the functional structure that Fayol had specified for a manufacturing business, that is, on engineering, manufacturing, selling, and so on; but it organized the business itself by the concept of federal decentralization, that is, on the basis of decentralized authority and centralized control. By the mid-1940s GM's structure had become the model for larger organizations around the world.

Where they fit the realities that confront organization designers and implementers today, the Fayol and Sloan models are still unsurpassed. Fayol's functional organization is still the best way to structure a small business, especially a small manufacturing business. Sloan's federal decentralization is still the best structure for the big, single-product, single-market company like GM. But more and more of the institutional reality that has to be structured and organized does not "fit." Indeed the very assumptions that underlay Sloan's work—and that of Fayol—are not applicable to today's organization challenges.

GM model vs. present realities

There are at least six ways in which the GM structure no longer serves as a model for present organization needs.

1. General Motors is a manufacturing business. Today we face the challenge of organizing the large nonmanufacturing institution. There are not only the large financial businesses and the large retailers, but also, equally, there are worldwide transportation, communications, and customer service companies. The latter, while they may manufacture a product, have their greatest emphasis on outside services (as most computer businesses do). Then there are, of course, all the nonbusiness service institutions, e.g., hospitals, universities, and government agencies. These "nonmanufacturing" institutions are, increasingly, the true center of gravity of any developed economy. They employ the most people, and they both contribute to and take the largest share of the gross national product. They present the fundamental organization problems today.

2. General Motors is essentially a single-product, single-technology, single-market business. Even accounting for the revenues of its large financial and insurance subsidiaries, four fifths of its total revenue are still produced by the automobile. Although Frigidaire and Electromo-

tive are large, important businesses and leaders in the consumer appliance and locomotive markets, respectively, they are but minor parts of GM. Indeed, GM is unique among large companies in being far less diversified today than it was 30 or 40 years ago. Then, in the late 1930s and early 1940s, General Motors had major investments in the chemical industry (Ethyl), in the aircraft industry (North American Aviation), and in earth-moving equipment (Euclid). All three are gone now and have not been replaced by new diversification activities outside the automotive field.

The cars that General Motors produces differ in details, such as size, horsepower, and price, but they are essentially one and the same product. A man who came up the line in, say, the Pontiac Division, will hardly find Chevrolet totally alien—and even Opel in Germany will not hold a great many surprises for him.

By contrast, the typical businesses of today are multiproduct, multitechnology, and multimarket. They may not be conglomerates, but they are diversified. And their central problem is a problem General Motors did not have: the organization of complexity and diversity.

There is, moreover, an even more difficult situation to which the GM pattern cannot be applied: the large single-product, single-technology business that, unlike GM, cannot be subdivided into distinct and yet comparable parts. Typical are the "materials" businesses such as steel and aluminum companies. Here belong, also, the larger transportation businesses, such as railroads, airlines, and the large commercial banks. These businesses are too big for a functional structure; it ceases to be a skeleton and becomes a straitjacket. They are also incapable of being genuinely decentralized; no one part on its own is a genuine "business." Yet as we are shifting from mechanical to process technologies, and from making goods to producing knowledge and services, these large, complex, but integrated businesses are becoming more important than the multidivisional businesses of the 1920s and 1930s.

3. General Motors still sees its international operations as organizationally separate and outside. For 50 years it has been manufacturing and selling overseas, and something like one quarter of its sales are now outside North America. But in its organization structure, in its reporting relationships, and above all in its career ladders,

GM is a U.S. company with foreign subsidiaries. Rather than leaning toward an international, let alone a multinational operation, GM's top management is primarily concerned with the U.S. market, the U.S. economy, the U.S. labor movement, the U.S. government, and so on. This traditional structure and viewpoint of GM's top management may, in large part, explain the substantial failure of GM to take advantage of the rapid expansion and growth of such major non-U.S. automobile markets as Europe, where GM's share has actually been dropping, or Brazil, where GM failed to anticipate a rapidly emerging automobile market.[1]

In contrast, during the last 20 years many other companies have become multinational. For these companies, a great many cultures, countries, markets, and governments are of equal, or at least of major, importance.

4. Because GM is a one-product, one-country company, information handling is not a major organization problem and thus not a major concern. At GM everyone speaks the same language, whether by that we mean the language of the automotive industry or American English. Everyone fully understands what the other one is doing or should be doing, if only because, in all likelihood, he has done a similar job himself. GM can, therefore, be organized according to the logic of the marketplace, and the logic of authority and decision. It need not, in its organization, concern itself a great deal with the logic and flow of information.

By contrast, multiproduct, multitechnology, and multinational companies have to design their organization structure to handle a large flow of information. At the very least they have to make sure that their organization structure does not violate the logic of information. And for this task, GM offers no guidance—GM did not have to tackle the problem.

5. Four out of every five GM employees are either manual production workers or clerks on routine tasks. In other words, GM employs yesterday's rather than today's labor force.

But the basic organization problem today concerns knowledge work and knowledge workers. They are the fastest growing element in every business; in service institutions, they are the core employees.

6. Finally, General Motors has been a "managerial" rather than an "entrepreneurial" business. The strength of the Sloan approach lay in its ability to manage, and manage superbly, what was already there and known.

1. For a discussion of these developments, see the epilogue to the new edition of my *Concept of the Corporation* (New York, John Day, 1972).

Today's organizer is challenged by an increasing demand to organize entrepreneurship and innovation. But for this undertaking, the General Motors model offers no guidance.

New design principles

We do not know how to handle these new organization realities or how to satisfy their structural demands. Nevertheless, the organizing task has not waited. To tackle the new realities, we have in the past 20 years improvised ad hoc design solutions to supplement the Fayol and Sloan models. As a result, the organization architect now has available five so-called design principles, i.e., five distinct organization structures. The two traditional ones already mentioned have been known as principles of organization design for many years:

○ Henri Fayol's functional structure.
○ Alfred P. Sloan's federal decentralization.

Three are new; indeed they are so new that they are not generally known, let alone recognized, as design principles:

○ Team organization.
○ Simulated decentralization.
○ Systems structure.

In team organization, a group—usually a fairly small one—is set up for a specific task rather than for a specific skill or stage in the work process. In the past 20 years we have learned that whereas team design was traditionally considered applicable only to short-lived, transitory, exceptional task-force assignments, it is equally applicable to some permanent needs, especially to the top-management and innovating tasks.

In an organization that is both too big to remain functionally organized and too integrated to be genuinely decentralized, simulated decentralization is often the organization answer. It sets up one function, one stage in the process, or one segment as if it were a distinct business with genuine profit and loss responsibility; it treats accounting fictions, transfer prices, and overhead allocations as if they were realities of the marketplace. For all its difficulties and frictions, simulated decentralization is probably the fastest growing organization design around these days. It is the only one that fits, albeit poorly,

the materials, computer, chemical, and pharmaceutical companies, as well as the big banks; it is also the only design principle suited for the large university, hospital, or government agency.

Finally, in systems structure, team organization and simulated decentralization are combined. The prototype for this design principle was NASA's space program, in which a large number of autonomous units—large government bodies, individual research scientists, profit-seeking businesses, and large universities—worked together, organized and informed by the needs of the situation rather than by logic, and held together by a common goal and a joint top management. The large transnational company, which is a mix of many cultures, governments, businesses, and markets, is the present embodiment of an organization based on the systems concept.

None of the new design principles is easy or trouble-free. Compared to the traditional designs of functionalism and federal decentralization, they are indeed so difficult, complex, and vulnerable that many organization theorists maintain that they are not principles at all, but abominations.[2] And there is no question that wherever the traditional principles can be used, they should be; they are infinitely easier. The traditional principles are, however, far more limited in their scope than the new ones, and when misapplied they can cause even greater problems.

Design logics

Each of the five design principles expresses or embodies a logic that makes that principle the appropriate one to apply when one or another task of management requires a structure. In this discussion we can identify three, or maybe four, logics upon which the five principles are based. For instance, although they do it differently, the functional and team design principles both embody *work* and *task* and are thus appropriate designs to consider when faced with work- or task-oriented management problems.

Historically these two design principles have been viewed as antithetical, but actually they are complementary. In the functionally organized structure, the work skills—manufacturing, accounting, and so on—are designed to be static; the work moves from one stage to others. In team structure, the work is conceived as static, with skills moving to meet the requirements of the task. Because of their complementary nature, these two design principles are the only possible choices for dealing with, say, the structure of

2. This is, for instance, the verdict of organization theorist Harold Koontz, in his well-publicized article, ''The Management Theory Jungle,'' *Journal of the Academy of Management*, December 1965; see also his ''Making Sense of Management Theory,'' HBR July-August 1962, p. 24.

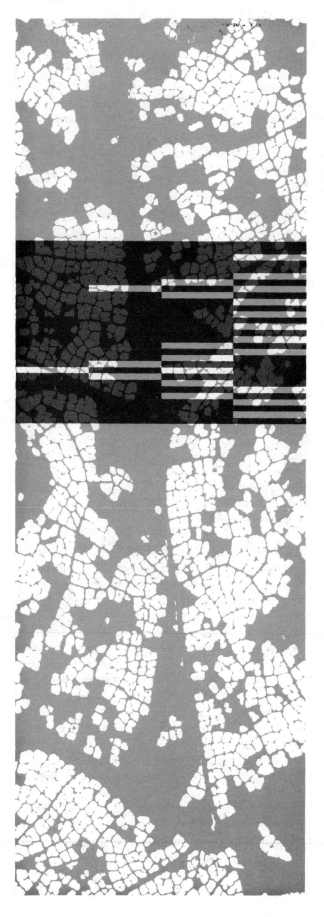

knowledge. For if you need a specific task performed and a team effort would do it best, then you need static functions as bases from which persons, and their expertise, can be moved to form a team.

Two other design logics, corresponding to those involving work and task, can also be defined. Simulated decentralization and Sloan's federal decentralization both deal with *results* and *performance*. They are result-focused designs. Unlike functional and team structures, however, they are not complementary; they are not even alternatives. Federal decentralization is an "optimum," simulated decentralization a "lesser evil" to be resorted to only when the stringent requirements of federal decentralization cannot be met.

The last of the available design principles, systems design, is focused on *relationships*, another dimension of management. Because relations are inevitably both more numerous and less clearly definable than either work and task or results, a structure focused on relations will present greater difficulties than either a work-focused or a result-focused design. There are, however, organization problems, as in the true multinational business, in which the very complexity of relationships makes systems design the only appropriate design principle.

This rough classification indicates that at least one additional design principle might yet be developed. *Decision* is as much a dimension of management as are work and task, results and performance, and relations. Yet, so far, we know of no decision-focused design principle of organization structure, but should one ever be developed, it might have wide applicability.[3]

Ideally, an organization should be multiaxial, that is, structured around work and task, *and* results and performance, *and* relationships, *and* decisions. It would function as if it were a biological organism, like the human body with its skeleton and muscles, a number of nervous systems, and with circulatory, digestive, immunological, and respiratory systems, all autonomous yet interdependent. But in social structures we are still limited to designs that express only one primary dimension.

So, in designing organizations, we have to choose among different structures, each stressing a different dimension and each, therefore, with distinct costs, specific and fairly stringent re-

3. Herbert A. Simon and his school have been attempting to develop one—at least this is how I read H.A. Simon's *Administrative Behavior* (New York, Macmillan, 1957) and I.G. March and H.A. Simon's *Organizations* (New York, John Wiley & Sons, 1958).

quirements, and real limitations. There is no risk-free organization structure. And a design that is the best solution for one task may be only one of a number of equally poor alternatives for another task, and just plain wrong for yet a third kind of work.

Major tasks of management

A somewhat different way of viewing the relationships between the design logics and principles is to identify the principal tasks of management that the principles can structure. We have learned that, in a very general analysis, organization design should simultaneously structure and integrate three different kinds of work: (1) the operating task, which is responsible for producing the results of today's business; (2) the innovative task, which creates the company's tomorrow; and (3) the top-management task, which directs, gives vision, and sets the course for the business of both today and tomorrow. No one organization design is adequate to all three kinds of work; every business will need to use several design principles side-by-side.

In addition, each organization structure has certain formal specifications that have nothing to do with the purpose of the structure but are integral parts of the structure itself. Just as a human body can be described as having certain characteristics, regardless of the occupation of its inhabitant, so can an organization structure. Bodies have arms and legs, hands and feet, all related to each other; similarly, organizations are structured to satisfy the need for:

O *Clarity*, as opposed to simplicity. (The Gothic cathedral is not a simple design, but your position inside it is clear; you know where to stand and where to go. A modern office building is exceedingly simple in design, but it is very easy to get lost in one; it is not clear.)

O *Economy* of effort to maintain control and minimize friction.

O *Direction of vision* toward the product rather than the process, the result rather than the effort.

O *Understanding* by each individual of his own task as well as that of the organization as a whole.

O *Decision making* that focuses on the right issues, is action-oriented, and is carried out at the lowest possible level of management.

O *Stability*, as opposed to rigidity, to survive turmoil, and *adaptability* to learn from it.

O *Perpetuation and self-renewal*, which require that an organization be able to produce tomorow's leaders from within, helping each person develop continuously; the structure must also be open to new ideas.

Even though every institution, and especially every business, is structured in some way around all the dimensions of management, no one design principle is adequate to all their demands and needs. Nor does any one of the five available design principles adequately satisfy all of the formal specifications. The functional principle, for instance, has great clarity and high economy, and it makes it easy to understand one's own task. But even in the small business it tends to direct vision away from results and toward efforts, to obscure the organization's goals, and to sub-optimize decisions. It has high stability but little adaptability. It perpetuates and develops technical and functional skills, that is, middle managers, but it resists new ideas and inhibits top-management development and vision. And every one of the other four principles is similarly both a "good fit" against some formal organization specifications and a "misfit" against others.

One conclusion from this discussion is that organization structures can either be pure or effective, but they are unlikely to be both. Indeed, even the purest structure we know of, Alfred Sloan's GM, was actually mixed. It was not composed just of decentralized divisions, with functional organization within the divisions. It also contained, from the beginning, some sizable simulated decentralization. For instance, Fisher Body had responsibility for all body work but not for any final product. And top management was clearly structured as a team, or rather as a number of interlocking teams.

This does not mean that an organization structure must by necessity be unwieldy or a confused mixture. The tremendous vitality of some older structures—Sears, Roebuck and GM, for instance—shows that a dynamic balance can be achieved. One implication is clear, however, and that is that pure structure *is* likely to end up badly botched. (This tendency may explain the difficulties that both GE and Imperial Chemicals—each trying for pure decentralization—have been experiencing.) Above all, our observations lead us to conclude that organization design is a series of risk-taking decisions rather than a search for the "one best way." And by and large, organization theorists and practitioners have yet to learn this.

Building the new structure

There are a number of important lessons to be learned from the previous discussion and from the experiences of the past 20 years. Some concern new ideas or conclusions we have not recognized before, while others involve rethinking old concepts and relationships that we thought were settled years ago.

The first thing we can conclude is that Fayol and Sloan were right: good organization structures will not just evolve. The only things that evolve by themselves in an organization are disorder, friction, and malperformance. Nor is the right structure—or even the livable one—intuitive, any more than Greek temples or Gothic cathedrals were. Traditions may indicate where the problems and malfunctions are, but they are of little help in finding solutions. Organization design and structure require thinking, analysis, and a systematic approach.

Second, we have learned that designing an organization structure is not the first step, but the last. The first step is to identify and organize the building blocks of organization, that is, the key tasks that have to be encompassed in the final structure and that, in turn, carry the structural load of the final edifice. This is, of course, what Fayol did with his functions of a manufacturing company, when he designed them according to the work to be done.

We now know that building blocks are determined by the kind of contribution they make. And we know that the traditional classification of the contributions, e.g., the staff-and-line concept of conventional U.S. organization theory, is more of a hindrance to understanding than a help.

Designing the building blocks or tasks is, so to speak, the "engineering phase" of organization design. It provides the basic materials. And like all materials, these building blocks have their specific characteristics. They belong in different places and fit together in different ways.

We have also learned that "structure follows strategy." Organization is not mechanical. It is not done by assembly, nor can it be prefabricated. Organization is organic and unique to

each individual business or institution. We realize now that structure is a means for attaining the objectives and goals of an institution. And if a structure is to be effective and sound, we must start with objectives and strategy.[4]

This is perhaps the most fruitful new insight we have in the field of organization. It may sound obvious, and it is. But some of the worst mistakes in organization building have been made by imposing on a living business a mechanistic model of an ideal organization.

Strategy—that is, the answer to the question: "What is our business? What should it be? What will it be?"—determines the purpose of structure. It thereby determines the key tasks or activities in a given business or service institution. Effective structure is the design that makes these key activities function and produce results. In turn the key activities are the load-bearing elements of a functioning structure. Organization design is, or should be, primarily concerned with the key activities; other purposes are secondary.

Some of the new insights into organization design require us to unlearn old ideas. A few of the noisiest and most time-consuming battles in organization theory and practice are pure sham. They pose an either/or dichotomy when the correct answer is "both—in varying proportions."

The first of these sham battles that had better be forgotten is between task-focus and person-focus in job design and organization structure. Structure and job design have to be task-focused. But assignments have to fit both the person and the needs of the situation. There is no point in confusing the two, as the old and tiresome discussion of the nonproblem insists on doing. Work is always objective and impersonal; the job itself is always done by a person.

Somewhat connected with this old controversy is the discussion of hierarchical versus free-form organization.

Traditional organization theory knows only one kind of structure, applicable alike to building blocks and whole buildings. It is the so-called scalar organization, that is, the hierarchical pyramid of superior and subordinates.

Today another—equally doctrinaire—organization theory is becoming fashionable. It maintains that shape and structure are what we want them to be—they are, or should be, free form. Everything—shape, size, and apparently tasks—derive from interpersonal relations. Indeed, it is argued, the purpose of the structure is to make it possible for each person "to do his thing."

4. The fundamental work on this topic, an in-depth study of the design of modern organization in pioneering American companies such as DuPont, General Motors, and Sears, was done by Alfred D. Chandler in his book *Strategy and Structure* (Cambridge, M.I.T. Press, 1962).

It is simply not true, however, that one of these forms represents total regimentation and the other total freedom. The amount of discipline required in both is the same; they only distribute it differently.

Hierarchy does not, as the critics allege, make the person at the top of the pyramid more powerful. On the contrary, the first effect of hierarchical organization is to protect the subordinate against arbitrary authority from above. A scalar or hierarchical organization does this by defining a sphere within which the subordinate has authority, a sphere within which the superior cannot interfere. It protects the subordinate by making it possible for him to say, "This is *my* assigned job." Protection of the subordinate also underlies the scalar principle's insistence that a man have only one superior. Otherwise, the subordinate is likely to find himself caught between conflicting demands, commands, interests, and loyalties. There is a lot of truth in the old proverb, "Better one bad master than two good ones."

At the same time, the hierarchical organization gives the most individual freedom. As long as the incumbent does whatever the assigned duties of his position are, he has done his job. He has no responsibility beyond it.

We hear a lot of talk these days about the individual's right to do his own thing. But the only organization structure in which this is remotely possible is a hierarchical one. It makes the least demands on the individual to subordinate himself to the goals of the organization or to gear his activities into the needs and demands of others.

Teams, by contrast, demand, above all, very great self-discipline from each member. Everybody has to do the team's "thing." Everybody has to take responsibility for the work of the entire team and for its performance. The one thing one cannot do on a team is one's own "thing."

Organization builders (and even organization theorists) will have to learn that sound organization structure needs both (a) a hierarchical structure of authority, and (b) a capacity to organize task forces, teams, and individuals for work on both a permanent and a temporary basis.

The 'one-way' myth

Organization theory and organization practice still assume that there is "one final answer," at least for a particular business or institution. In itself, this belief is a large part of today's organization crisis. It leads to doctrinaire structures that impose one template on everybody and everything—e.g., operating and innovating components; manufacturing and service units; single-product and multimarket businesses. And if any person or process, no matter how insignificant, seems out of place, a total root-and-branch reorganization has to be done to accommodate it.

Maybe there is one right answer—but if so, we do not yet have it. Indeed for certain businesses and institutions, such as a large airline or government agency, we do not even have one poor answer—all we have are a multitude of equally unsatisfactory approaches. But, as remarked before, the organizing task will not wait; it will by necessity continue to be a central preoccupation of managers. Therefore, they had better learn to understand the design principles we already have. They must also learn the formal specifications of organization, and the relationships between the tasks of a business and the structures available to it.

The true lesson of the organization crisis is, however, quite different. It is that the traditional quest for the one right answer—a quest pursued as wholeheartedly by the new "heretics" of free-form organization as by the most orthodox classicists—pursues the wrong quarry. It misconceives an organization as something in itself rather than as a means to an end. But now we can see that liberation and mobilization of human energies—rather than symmetry, harmony, or consistency—are the purpose of organization. Human performance is both its goal and its test.

Reprint 74102

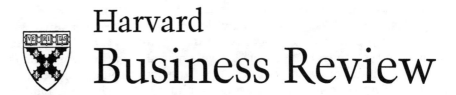

Peter F. Drucker

Management's new role

*What are the big tasks waiting
for management today that require both
new theories and new practices?*

Foreword

While we are not overnight going to abandon the traditional assumptions that practitioners and theoreticians alike still take for granted, these are nonetheless rapidly being invalidated or rendered obsolete. This article identifies the five new and different assumptions about management that correspond to today's realities and provide better guides to effectively dealing with the scope, the task, the position, and the nature of management.

Mr. Drucker is Professor of Management at the Graduate School of Business Administration of New York University. As a teacher, scholar, consultant, and writer, he specializes in business and economic policy and in top management organization.

The major assumptions on which both the theory and the practice of management have been based these past 50 years are rapidly becoming inappropriate. A few of these assumptions are actually no longer valid and, in fact, are obsolete. Others, while still applicable, are fast becoming inadequate; they deal with what is increasingly the secondary, the subordinate, the exceptional, rather than the primary, the dominant, and the ruling function and reality of management.

To a considerable extent, the obsolescence and inadequacy of these assumed "verities" of management reflect management's own success. For management has been the success story par excellence of these last 50 years—more so even than science. But to an even greater extent, the tradi-

Author's note: This article is adapted from a keynote address to be delivered at the 15th CIOS International Management Congress in Tokyo, Japan, on November 7, 1969.

tional assumptions are being outmoded by independent—or at least only partially dependent—new developments in our society, in our economy, and in the world view of our age, especially in the industrialized countries. To a large extent, objective reality is changing around the manager's basic role—and fast.

Managers everywhere are very conscious of new concepts and new tools of management, of new concepts of organization, and of the "information revolution." These changes within management are indeed of great importance. But more important yet may be the changes in the basic realities and their impact on the fundamental assumptions underlying management as a theory and as a practice. The changes in managerial concepts and tools will force managers to change their behavior. The changes in concepts and tools mean a change in what a manager *does* and how he *does* it. The changes in reality demand, however, a change in the manager's role. And a change in his basic role means a change in what a manager *is*.

In this article, I shall first briefly mention the traditional assumptions that most men of management—practitioners and theoreticians alike—still take for granted. Then I shall attempt to formulate different ones that correspond to the management realities of today.

The old assumptions . . .

In my considered judgment, there are five assumptions that may have formed the foundation of the theory and practice of management in the last half century. These assumptions deal with the scope, the task, the position, and the nature of management.

Of course, few practitioners of management have ever been conscious of them. Even the management scholars have, as a rule, rarely stated them explicitly. But both practitioners and theorists alike have accepted these assumptions, have indeed treated them as self-evident axioms, and have based their theories and actions on them.

Number one

Only business has "social responsibility."

This view derives directly from the belief—which is widely held, although not necessarily by business—that business is the one exceptional institution. According to this belief, the university or hospital is not assumed to have any social responsibility, primarily because of not being within the purview of the traditional vision. In other words, neither the university nor the hospital is seen at all as an "organization." Moreover, the traditional view of a social responsibility peculiar and confined to business derives from the premise that economic activity differs drastically from these other human activities.

Number two

Entrepreneurship and innovation lie outside the management scope.

This assumption takes the view that the primary, and perhaps the only, task of management is to mobilize the energies of the business organization for the accomplishment of known and defined tasks.

To a large extent this assumption was a necessity during the last half century. The concern of the world of 1900 was the large and complex organization for production and distribution with which the traditional managerial systems, whether of the workshop or of the local store, could not cope.

Thus the invention of the steam locomotive was not what triggered concern with management. Rather, it was the emergence some 50 years later of the large railroad company, which could handle steam locomotives without much trouble, but was baffled by the problem of coordination and communication between people and by the problem of separation of their authorities and responsibilities.

But the focus on the *managerial* side of management—to the almost total neglect of entrepreneurship as a function of management—also reflects the reality of the economy in the half century since World War I. It was a period of high technological and entrepreneurial continuity—a period which required adaptation rather than innovation, and ability to do better rather than courage to do differently.

Number three

It is management's task to make the manual worker productive.

The manual worker—skilled or unskilled—has been management's concern as a resource, as a cost center, and as a social and individual problem.

Thus to have made the manual worker productive is indeed the greatest achievement of management to date. Frederick Winslow Taylor's *Scientific Management* is often attacked these days (though mostly by people who have not read it). But it was his insistence on studying work that underlies the affluence of today's developed countries; it raised the productivity of manual work to the point where yesterday's laborer has become the semiskilled worker of today's mass production industries with a middle-class standard of living and guaranteed job or income security.

As late as World War II, the central concern was still the productivity and management of manual work; the central achievement of both the British and the American war economies was the mobilization, training, and management of production workers in large numbers. Even in the postwar period one major task—in all developed countries other than Great Britain—was the rapid conversion of immigrants from the farm into productive manual workers in industry. On this accomplishment—made possible only because of the scientific management which Taylor pioneered 70 years ago—largely rest the economic growth and performance of Japan, of Western Europe, and even of the United States.

Number four

Management is a "science" or at least a "discipline."

This assumption is based on two propositions. The first is that management is as independent of cultural values and individual beliefs as are the elementary operations of arithmetic, the laws of physics, or the stress tables of the engineer. The other is that all management is being practiced within one distinct national environment and embedded in one national culture, circumscribed by one legal code and part of one national economy.

These two propositions were as obvious to Taylor in the United States as they were to Fayol in France. Of all the early management authorities, only Rathenau in Germany seems to have doubted that management was a culture-free discipline—and no one listened to him. The human relations people attacked Taylor as "unscientific"; they did not attack Taylor's premise that there was an objective science of management. On the contrary, they proclaimed their findings to be "true" scientific psychology and grounded in the "nature of man." They refused even to take into account the findings of their

own colleagues in the social sciences, the cultural anthropologists. Insofar as cultural factors were considered at all in the traditional assumptions about management, these were regarded as "obstacles."

Number five

Management is the result of economic development.

This assumption holds that management is a result rather than a cause, and a response to needs rather than a creator of opportunity.

Of course, this had been the historical experience of the West, but even in the West the traditional explanation of the emergence of management was largely myth. As the textbooks had

it (and still largely have it), management came into being when the small business outgrew the owner who had done everything himself.

In reality, management evolved in enterprises that started big and could never have been anything but big—the railways in particular, but also the postal service, the steamship companies, the steel mills, and the department stores. To industries that could start small, management came very late; some of those (e.g., the textile mill or the bank) are still often run on the pattern of the "one boss" who does everything and who, at best, has "helpers."

I fully realize that I have oversimplified, but I do not believe that I have misrepresented our traditional assumptions. Nor do I believe that I am mistaken in thinking that these assumptions, in one form or another, still underlie both the theory and the practice of management, especially in the industrially developed nations.

. . . vs. *the new realities*

Today we need quite different assumptions—more in keeping with today's realities than the assumptions on which theory and practice of management have been basing themselves these past 50 years.

Here, in this section of the article, I shall attempt to present corresponding new assumptions. These, too, are oversimplified—grossly so. They are far closer to the realities of our time, however.

Number one

All institutions, including business, are accountable for the "quality of life."

Because our society is rapidly becoming a society of organizations, all institutions will have to make fulfillment of basic social values, beliefs, and purposes a major objective of their continuing activities rather than a social responsibility that restrains or lies outside their primary functions. In the business enterprise, this means that attainment of the quality of life will increasingly have to be (a) considered a business opportunity and (b) converted by management into profitable business.

This will apply particularly to fulfillment of the individual. It will increasingly be the job of management to make the individual's values and aspirations redound to organizational energy and performance. It will simply not be good enough to be satisfied—as industrial relations and even human relations traditionally have been—with the absence of discontent.

Perhaps one way to dramatize this is to say that we will, within another 10 years, become far less concerned with *management* development (that is, adapting the individual to the demands of the organization), and far more with *organization* development (that is, adapting the company to the needs, aspirations, and potentials of individuals).

Number two

Entrepreneurial innovation will become the very heart and core of management.

There is little doubt in my mind that entrepreneurial innovation will be as important to

management in the future as the managerial function itself is currently. Indeed, it may be more important in the years to come. Unlike the nineteenth century, however, entrepreneurial innovation will increasingly have to be carried out in, and by, existing institutions, such as on-going businesses. It will, therefore, no longer be possible to consider it as lying outside management or even as being peripheral to management.

There is every reason to believe that the closing decades of the twentieth century will see changes as rapid as those that characterized the 50-odd years between 1860 and 1914, when a new major invention, ushering in almost immediately a new major industry with new big businesses, appeared on the scene every two to three years on average.[1] Unlike the last century, however, these innovations of ours will be as much social as technical; a metropolis, for instance, is clearly as much of a challenge to the innovator today as the new science of electricity was to the inventor of 1870. And also, unlike the last century, innovation in this century will increasingly be based on knowledge of all kinds rather than on science alone.

At the same time, innovation will increasingly have to be channeled in and through existing businesses, if only because the tax laws in every developed country make the existing business the center of capital accumulation. And innovation is capital-intensive, especially in the two crucial phases of development and market introduction of new products, new processes, or new services.

We will, therefore, increasingly have to learn to make existing organizations capable of rapid and continuing innovation. How far we are from this is shown by the fact that management still worries about resistance to change. Existing organizations will have to learn to reach out for change as an opportunity, will have to learn to resist continuity.

Number three

It is management's task to make knowledge more productive.

The basic capital resource, the fundamental investment, and the cost center of a developed economy all rest in the application of knowledge—that is, in concepts, ideas, and theories—rather than in manual skill or muscle.

1. For documentation, see my recent book, *The Age of Discontinuity* (New York, Harper & Row, 1969).

Taylor put knowledge to work to make the manual worker productive. But Taylor himself never asked the question: What constitutes "productivity" with respect to the industrial engineer who applies scientific management? As a result of Taylor's work, we can answer what productivity is with respect to the manual worker. But we still cannot answer what productivity is with respect to the industrial engineer or to any other knowledge worker.

Surely, the measurements which give us productivity for the manual worker, such as the number of pieces turned out per hour or per dollar of wages, are quite irrelevant if applied to the knowledge worker. There are few things as useless and unproductive as the engineering department that with great dispatch, industry, and elegance turns out the drawings for an unsalable product. The productivity of the knowledge worker is primarily a matter not of quantity but of quality. We cannot even define it yet.

One thing is clear: to make knowledge productive will bring about changes in job structure, careers, and organizations as drastic as those which resulted in the factory from the application of scientific management to manual work. The entrance job will, above all, have to be changed drastically to enable the knowledge worker to become productive. For it is abundantly clear that knowledge cannot be productive unless the worker finds out who he himself is, what kind of work he is fitted for, and how he works best.

In other words, there can be no divorce of *planning* from *doing* in knowledge work. On the contrary, the knowledge worker must be able to plan himself. And this the present entrance jobs, by and large, do not make possible. They are based on the assumption—valid for manual work but quite inappropriate to knowledge work —that anyone can objectively determine the "one best way" for any kind of work. For knowledge work, this is simply not true. There may be one best way, but it is heavily conditioned by the individual and is not entirely determined by physical (or even mental) characteristics of the job. It is temperamental as well.

Number four

Management will have to be considered as both a "science" and a "humanity."

There are management tools and techniques; there are management concepts and principles. There is a common language of management,

and there may even be a universal discipline of management. Certainly, there is a worldwide generic function which we call "management," and which serves the same purpose in any and all developed society.

But management is also a culture and a system of values and beliefs. It is also the means through which a given society makes productive its own values and beliefs. Management may well be considered the bridge between a *civilization* which is rapidly becoming worldwide, and a *culture* which expresses divergent traditions, values, beliefs, and heritages. Management must become the instrument through which cultural diversity can be made to serve the common purposes of mankind.

At the same time, management increasingly is being practiced not within the confines of one national culture, law, or sovereignty but "multinationally." Indeed, management increasingly is becoming an institution—so far, the only one —of a genuine world economy.

Management, we now know, has to make productive the values, aspirations, and traditions of the individual, the community, and the society for a common productive purpose. If management does not succeed in putting to work the specific cultural heritage of a country and of a people, social and economic development cannot take place. This is, of course, the great lesson of Japan—and the fact that Japan a century ago put to work her own traditions of community and human values for the new ends of a modern industrial economy explains why Japan succeeded while every other non-Western country has so far failed.

As a science and a humanity, management is both a statement of findings that can be objectively tested and validated and a system of belief and experience.

At the same time, management—and here I mean business management alone, so far—is rapidly emerging as the one and only institution that is common and transcends the boundaries of the national state. The "multinational corporation" does not really exist so far. Rather, what we have, by and large, are businesses that are based on one country with one culture and, for the most part, one nationality, especially in top management. But it is also becoming clear that this is a transition phenomenon and that continuing development of the world economy both requires and leads to genuinely multinational companies, in which not only are production and sales multinational, but ownership and management as well—all the way from the top down.

Within the individual country, especially the developed country, business is rapidly losing its exceptional status as we recognize that it is the prototype of the typical (indeed, the universal) social form, the organized institution requiring management. Beyond the national boundary, however, business is rapidly acquiring the same exceptional status it no longer has within the individual developed country, is rapidly becoming the unique, the exceptional, the one institution that expresses the reality of a world economy and of a worldwide knowledge society.

Number five

Economic and social development are the result of management.

It can be said without too much oversimplification that there are no underdeveloped countries. There are only *undermanaged* ones. Japan 100 years ago was an underdeveloped country by every material measurement. But it very quickly built up management of great competence, indeed of excellence. Within 25 years, Meiji Japan had become a developed country and indeed in some aspects, such as literacy, the most highly developed of all countries. We realize today that it is Meiji Japan, rather than eighteenth-century England—or even nineteenth-century Germany—which has to be the model of development for the underdeveloped world.

All our experience in economic development proves that management is the prime mover and that development is a consequence. Wherever we have only contributed the economic factors of production, especially capital, we have not achieved development. In the few cases where we have been able to generate management energies (e.g., in the Cauca Valley in Colombia), we have generated rapid development, which is a matter of human energies rather than of economic wealth. And the generation and direction of human energies is the task of management.

Conclusion

I submit that the new assumptions about management that I have discussed in this article are better guides to effective management in the developed countries today, let alone tomorrow,

than the assumptions on which we have based our theories, as well as our practices, these last 50 years.

Not that we are going to abandon the old tasks. Obviously, we still have to manage the existing enterprise and create internal order and organization. We still have to manage the manual worker and make him productive. And no one who knows the reality of management is likely to assert that we know everything in these and similar areas that we need to know.

But the big jobs waiting for management today, the big tasks requiring both new theory and new practice, arise out of new realities and demand different assumptions and approaches.

More important even than the new tasks may be management's new role. Management is fast becoming the central resource of the developed countries and the basic need of the developing ones. From being the specific concern of one (i.e., the economic institutions of society), management and managers are becoming the generic, the distinctive, the constitutive organ of developed society. What management is and what managers do will therefore —and properly—increasingly become a matter of public concern rather than a matter for the "experts." Management will increasingly be concerned as much with the expression of basic beliefs and values as with the accomplishment of measurable results. It will increasingly stand for the quality of life of a society as much as for its standard of living.

There are many new tools of management whose use we will have to learn, and many new techniques. There are, as I have pointed out, a great many new and difficult tasks. But the most important change ahead for management is that increasingly the aspirations, the values, and indeed the very survival of society in the developed countries will come to depend on the performance, the competence, and the values of managers. The task of the next generation is to make productive for the individual, the community, and the society the new organized institutions of our new pluralism. And that is, above all, *management's new role.*

Reprint 69605

The Effective Decision

. . . results from a systematic process, with clearly defined elements, that is handled in a distinct sequence of steps.

By Peter F. Drucker

Effective executives do not make a great many decisions. They concentrate on what is important. They try to make the few important decisions on the highest level of conceptual understanding. They try to find the constants in a situation, to think through what is strategic and generic rather than to "solve problems." They are, therefore, not overly impressed by speed in decision making; rather, they consider virtuosity in manipulating a great many variables a symptom of sloppy thinking. They want to know what the decision is all about and what the underlying realities are which it has to satisfy. They want impact rather than technique. And they want to be sound rather than clever.

Effective executives know when a decision has to be based on principle and when it should be made pragmatically, on the merits of the case. They know the trickiest decision is that between the right and the wrong compromise, and they have learned to tell one from the other. They know that the most time-consuming step in the process is not making the decision but putting it into effect. Unless a decision has "degenerated into work," it is not a decision; it is at best a good intention. This means that, while the effective decision itself is based on the highest level of conceptual understanding, the action commitment should be as close as possible to the capacities of the people who have to carry it out. Above all, effective execu-tives know that decision making has its own systematic process and its own clearly defined elements.

Sequential Steps

The elements do not by themselves "make" the decisions. Indeed, every decision is a risk-taking judgment. But unless these elements are the stepping-stones of the executive's decision process, he will not arrive at a right, and certainly not at an effective, decision. Therefore, in this article I shall describe the sequence of steps involved in the decision-making process. There are six such steps:

1. *The classification of the problem.* Is it generic? Is it exceptional and unique? Or is it the first manifestation of a new genus for which a rule has yet to be developed?

2. *The definition of the problem.* What are we dealing with?

3. *The specifications which the answer to the problem must satisfy.* What are the "boundary conditions"?

4. *The decision as to what is "right," rather than what is acceptable, in order to meet the boundary conditions.* What will fully satisfy the specifications *before* attention is given to the compromises, adaptations, and concessions needed to make the decision acceptable?

AUTHOR'S NOTE: This article is derived from a chapter in my forthcoming book, *The Effective Executive*, to be published by Harper & Row, Publishers, Inc.

5. *The building into the decision of the action to carry it out.* What does the action commitment have to be? Who has to know about it?

6. *The feedback which tests the validity and effectiveness of the decision against the actual course of events.* How is the decision being carried out? Are the assumptions on which it is based appropriate or obsolete?

Let us take a look at each of these individual elements.

The Classification

The effective decision maker asks: Is this a symptom of a fundamental disorder or a stray event? The generic always has to be answered through a rule, a principle. But the truly exceptional event can only be handled as such and as it comes.

Strictly speaking, the executive might distinguish among four, rather than between two, different types of occurrences.

First, there is the truly generic event, of which the individual occurrence is only a symptom. Most of the "problems" that come up in the course of the executive's work are of this nature. Inventory decisions in a business, for instance, are not "decisions." They are adaptations. The problem is generic. This is even more likely to be true of occurrences within manufacturing organizations. For example:

A product control and engineering group will typically handle many hundreds of problems in the course of a month. Yet, whenever these are analyzed, the great majority prove to be just symptoms — and manifestations — of underlying basic situations. The individual process control engineer or production engineer who works in one part of the plant usually cannot see this. He might have a few problems each month with the couplings in the pipes that carry steam or hot liquids, and that's all.

Only when the total workload of the group over several months is analyzed does the generic problem appear. Then it is seen that temperatures or pressures have become too great for the existing equipment and that the couplings holding the various lines together need to be redesigned for greater loads. Until this analysis is done, process control will spend a tremendous amount of time fixing leaks without ever getting control of the situation.

The second type of occurrence is the problem which, while a unique event for the individual institution, is actually generic. Consider:

The company that receives an offer to merge from another, larger one, will never receive such an offer again if it accepts. This is a nonrecurrent situation as far as the individual company, its board of directors, and its management are concerned. But it is, of course, a generic situation which occurs all the time. Thinking through whether to accept or to reject the offer requires some general rules. For these, however, the executive has to look to the experience of others.

Next there is the truly exceptional event that the executive must distinguish. To illustrate:

The huge power failure that plunged into darkness the whole of Northeastern North America from the St. Lawrence to Washington in November 1965 was, according to first explanations, a truly exceptional situation. So was the thalidomide tragedy which led to the birth of so many deformed babies in the early 1960's. The probability of either of these events occurring, we were told, was one in ten million or one in a hundred million, and concatenations of these events were as unlikely ever to recur again as it is unlikely, for instance, for the chair on which I sit to disintegrate into its constituent atoms.

Truly unique events are rare, however. Whenever one appears, the decision maker has to ask: Is this a true exception or only the first manifestation of a new genus? And this — the early manifestation of a new generic problem — is the fourth and last category of events with which the decision process deals. Thus:

We know now that both the Northeastern power failure and the thalidomide tragedy were only the first occurrences of what, under conditions of modern power technology or of modern pharmacology, are likely to become fairly frequent occurrences unless generic solutions are found.

All events but the truly unique require a generic solution. They require a rule, a policy, or a principle. Once the right principle has been developed, all manifestations of the same generic situation can be handled pragmatically — that is, by adaptation of the rule to the concrete circumstances of the case. Truly unique events, however, must be treated individually. The executive cannot develop rules for the exceptional.

The effective decision maker spends time determining with which of the four different types of the above situations he is dealing. He knows that he will make the wrong decision if he classifies the situation incorrectly.

By far the most common mistake of the decision maker is to treat a generic situation as if it were a series of unique events — that is, to be pragmatic when lacking the generic understanding and principle. The inevitable result is frustration and futility. This was clearly shown, I think, by the failure of most of the policies, both domestic and foreign, of the Kennedy Administration. Consider:

For all the brilliance of its members, the Administration achieved fundamentally only one success, and that was in the Cuban missile crisis. Otherwise, it achieved practically nothing. The main reason was surely what its members called "pragmatism" — namely, the Administration's refusal to develop rules and principles, and its insistence on treating everything "on its merits." Yet it was clear to everyone, including the members of the Administration, that the basic assumptions on which its policies rested — the valid assumptions of the immediate postwar years — had become increasingly unrealistic in international, as well as in domestic, affairs in the 1960's.

Equally common is the mistake of treating a new event as if it were just another example of the old problem to which, therefore, the old rules should be applied:

This was the error that snowballed the local power failure on the New York-Ontario border into the great Northeastern blackout. The power engineers, especially in New York City, applied the right rule for a normal overload. Yet their own instruments had signaled that something quite extraordinary was going on which called for exceptional, rather than standard, countermeasures.

By contrast, the one great triumph of President Kennedy in the Cuban missile crisis rested on acceptance of the challenge to think through an extraordinary, exceptional occurrence. As soon as he accepted this, his own tremendous resources of intelligence and courage effectively came into play.

The Definition

Once a problem has been classified as generic or unique, it is usually fairly easy to define. "What is this all about?" "What is pertinent here?" "What is the key to this situation?" Questions such as these are familiar. But only the truly effective decision makers are aware that the danger in this step is not the wrong definition; it is the plausible but incomplete one. For example:

The American automobile industry held to a plausible but incomplete definition of the prob-

lem of automotive safety. It was this lack of awareness — far more than any reluctance to spend money on safety engineering — that eventually, in 1966, brought the industry under sudden and sharp Congressional attack for its unsafe cars and then left the industry totally bewildered by the attack. It simply is not true that the industry has paid scant attention to safety.

On the contrary, it has worked hard at safer highway engineering and at driver training, believing these to be the major areas for concern. That accidents are caused by unsafe roads and unsafe drivers is plausible enough. Indeed, all other agencies concerned with automotive safety, from the highway police to the high schools, picked the same targets for their campaigns. These campaigns have produced results. The number of accidents on highways built for safety has been greatly lessened. Similarly, safety-trained drivers have been involved in far fewer accidents.

But although the ratio of accidents per thousand cars or per thousand miles driven has been going down, the total number of accidents and the severity of them have kept creeping up. It should therefore have become clear long ago that something would have to be done about the small but significant probability that accidents will occur despite safety laws and safety training.

This means that future safety campaigns will have to be supplemented by engineering to make accidents themselves less dangerous. Whereas cars have been engineered to be safe when used correctly, they will also have to be engineered for safety when used incorrectly.

There is only one safeguard against becoming the prisoner of an incomplete definition: check it again and again against *all* the observable facts, and throw out a definition the moment it fails to encompass any of them.

The effective decision maker always tests for signs that something is atypical or something unusual is happening. He always asks: Does the definition explain the observed events, and does it explain all of them? He always writes out what the definition is expected to make happen — for instance, make automobile accidents disappear — and then tests regularly to see if this really happens. Finally, he goes back and thinks the problem through again whenever he sees something atypical, when he finds phenomena his explanation does not really explain, or when the course of events deviates, even in details, from his expectations.

These are in essence the rules Hippocrates laid down for medical diagnosis well over 2,000 years ago. They are the rules for scientific observation first formulated by Aristotle and then reaffirmed by Galileo 300 years ago. These, in other words, are old, well-known, time-tested rules, which an executive can learn and apply systematically.

The Specifications

The next major element in the decision process is defining clear specifications as to what the decision has to accomplish. What are the objectives the decision has to reach? What are the minimum goals it has to attain? What are the conditions it has to satisfy? In science these are known as "boundary conditions." A decision, to be effective, needs to satisfy the boundary conditions. Consider:

"Can our needs be satisfied," Alfred P. Sloan, Jr. presumably asked himself when he took command of General Motors in 1922, "by removing the autonomy of our division heads?" His answer was clearly in the negative. The boundary conditions of his problem demanded strength and responsibility in the chief operating positions. This was needed as much as unity and control at the center. Everyone before Sloan had seen the problem as one of personalities — to be solved through a struggle for power from which one man would emerge victorious. The boundary conditions, Sloan realized, demanded a solution to a constitutional problem — to be solved through a new structure: decentralization which balanced local autonomy of operations with central control of direction and policy.

A decision that does not satisfy the boundary conditions is worse than one which wrongly defines the problem. It is all but impossible to salvage the decision that starts with the right premises but stops short of the right conclusions. Furthermore, clear thinking about the boundary conditions is needed to know when a decision has to be abandoned. The most common cause of failure in a decision lies not in its being wrong initially. Rather, it is a subsequent shift in the goals — the specifications — which makes the prior right decision suddenly inappropriate. And unless the decision maker has kept the boundary conditions clear, so as to make possible the immediate replacement of the outflanked decision with a new and appropriate policy, he may not even notice that things have changed. For example:

Franklin D. Roosevelt was bitterly attacked for his switch from conservative candidate in 1932 to radical President in 1933. But it wasn't Roosevelt who changed. The sudden economic collapse which occurred between the summer of 1932 and the spring of 1933 changed the specifications. A policy appropriate to the goal of national economic recovery — which a conservative economic policy might have been — was no longer appropriate when, with the Bank Holiday, the goal had to become political and social cohesion. When the boundary conditions changed, Roosevelt immediately substituted a political objective (reform) for his former economic one (recovery).

Above all, clear thinking about the boundary conditions is needed to identify the most dangerous of all possible decisions: the one in which the specifications that have to be satisfied are essentially incompatible. In other words, this is the decision that might — just might — work if nothing whatever goes wrong. A classic case is President Kennedy's Bay of Pigs decision:

One specification was clearly Castro's overthrow. The other was to make it appear that the invasion was a "spontaneous" uprising of the Cubans. But these two specifications would have been compatible with each other only if an immediate island-wide uprising against Castro would have completely paralyzed the Cuban army. And while this was not impossible, it clearly was not probable in such a tightly controlled police state.

Decisions of this sort are usually called "gambles." But actually they arise from something much less rational than a gamble — namely, a hope against hope that two (or more) clearly incompatible specifications can be fulfilled simultaneously. This is hoping for a miracle; and the trouble with miracles is not that they happen so rarely, but that they are, alas, singularly unreliable.

Everyone can make the wrong decision. In fact, everyone will sometimes make a wrong decision. But no executive needs to make a decision which, on the face of it, seems to make sense but, in reality, falls short of satisfying the boundary conditions.

The Decision

The effective executive has to start out with what is "right" rather than what is acceptable precisely because he always has to compromise in the end. But if he does not know what will satisfy the boundary conditions, the decision maker cannot distinguish between the right compromise and the wrong compromise — and may end up by making the wrong compromise. Consider:

I was taught this when I started in 1944 on my first big consulting assignment. It was a study of the management structure and policies of General Motors Corporation. Alfred P. Sloan, Jr., who was then chairman and chief executive officer of the company, called me to his office at the start of my assignment and said: "I shall not tell you what to study, what to write, or what conclusions to come to. This is your task. My only instruction to you is to put down what you think is right as you see it. Don't you worry about our reaction. Don't you worry about whether we will like this or dislike that. And don't you, above all, concern yourself with the compromises that might be needed to make your conclusions acceptable. There is not one executive in this company who does not know how to make every single conceivable compromise without any help from you. But he can't make the *right* compromise unless you first tell him what right is."

The effective executive knows that there are two different kinds of compromise. One is expressed in the old proverb: "Half a loaf is better than no bread." The other, in the story of the Judgment of Solomon, is clearly based on the realization that "half a baby is worse than no baby at all." In the first instance, the boundary conditions are still being satisfied. The purpose of bread is to provide food, and half a loaf is still food. Half a baby, however, does not satisfy the boundary conditions. For half a baby is not half of a living and growing child.

It is a waste of time to worry about what will be acceptable and what the decision maker should or should not say so as not to evoke resistance. (The things one worries about seldom happen, while objections and difficulties no one thought about may suddenly turn out to be almost insurmountable obstacles.) In other words, the decision maker gains nothing by starting out with the question: "What is acceptable?" For in the process of answering it, he usually gives away the important things and loses any chance to come up with an effective — let alone the right — answer.

The Action

Converting the decision into action is the fifth major element in the decision process. While thinking through the boundary conditions is the most difficult step in decision making, converting the decision into effective action is usually the most time-consuming one. Yet a decision will not become effective unless the action commitments have been built into it from the start.

In fact, no decision has been made unless carrying it out in specific steps has become someone's work assignment and responsibility. Until then, it is only a good intention.

The flaw in so many policy statements, especially those of business, is that they contain no action commitment — to carry them out is no one's specific work and responsibility. Small wonder then that the people in the organization tend to view such statements cynically, if not as declarations of what top management is really *not* going to do.

Converting a decision into action requires answering several distinct questions: Who has to know of this decision? What action has to be taken? Who is to take it? What does the action have to be so that the people who have to do it *can* do it? The first and the last of these questions are too often overlooked — with dire results. A story that has become a legend among operations researchers illustrates the importance of the question, "Who has to know?":

A major manufacturer of industrial equipment decided several years ago to discontinue one of its models that had for years been standard equipment on a line of machine tools, many of which were still in use. It was, therefore, decided to sell the model to present owners of the old equipment for another three years as a replacement, and then to stop making and selling it. Orders for this particular model had been going down for a good many years. But they shot up immediately as customers reordered against the day when the model would no longer be available. No one had, however, asked, "Who needs to know of this decision?"

Consequently, nobody informed the purchasing clerk who was in charge of buying the parts from which the model itself was being assembled. His instructions were to buy parts in a given ratio to current sales — and the instructions remained unchanged.

Thus, when the time came to discontinue further production of the model, the company had in its warehouse enough parts for another 8 to 10 years of production, parts that had to be written off at a considerable loss.

The action must also be appropriate to the capacities of the people who have to carry it out. Thus:

A large U.S. chemical company found itself, in recent years, with fairly large amounts of blocked currency in two West African countries. To protect this money, top management decided to invest it locally in businesses which (a) would contribute to the local economy, (b) would not require imports from abroad, and (c) would if successful be the kind that could be sold to local investors if and when currency remittances became possible again. To establish these businesses, the company developed a simple chemical process to preserve a tropical fruit — a staple crop in both countries — which, up until then, had suffered serious spoilage in transit to its Western markets.

The business was a success in both countries. But in one country the local manager set the business up in such a manner that it required highly skilled and technically trained management of a kind not easily available in West Africa. In the other country the local manager thought through the capacities of the people who would eventually have to run the business. Consequently, he worked hard at making both the process and the business simple, and at staffing his operation from the start with local nationals right up to the top management level.

A few years later it became possible again to transfer currency from these two countries. But, though the business flourished, no buyer could be found for it in the first country. No one available locally had the necessary managerial and technical skills to run it, and so the business had to be liquidated at a loss. In the other country so many local entrepreneurs were eager to buy the business that the company repatriated its original investment with a substantial profit.

The chemical process and the business built on it were essentially the same in both places. But in the first country no one had asked: "What kind of people do we have available to make this decision effective? And what can they do?" As a result, the decision itself became frustrated.

This action commitment becomes doubly important when people have to change their behavior, habits, or attitudes if a decision is to become effective. Here, the executive must make sure not only that the responsibility for the action is clearly assigned, but that the people assigned are capable of carrying it out. Thus the decision maker has to make sure that the measurements, the standards for accomplishment, and the incentives of those charged with the action responsibility are changed simultaneously. Otherwise, the organization people will get caught in a paralyzing internal emotional conflict. Consider these two examples:

❡ When Theodore Vail was president of the Bell Telephone System 60 years ago, he decided that the business of the Bell System was service. This decision explains in large part why the United States (and Canada) has today an investor-owned,

rather than a nationalized, telephone system. Yet this policy statement might have remained a dead letter if Vail had not at the same time designed yardsticks of service performance and introduced these as a means to measure, and ultimately to reward, managerial performance. The Bell managers of that time were used to being measured by the profitability (or at least by the cost) of their units. The new yardsticks resulted in the rapid acceptance of the new objectives.

❡ In sharp contrast is the recent failure of a brilliant chairman and chief executive to make effective a new organization structure and new objectives in an old, large, and proud U.S. company. Everyone agreed that the changes were needed. The company, after many years as leader of its industry, showed definite signs of aging. In many markets newer, smaller, and more aggressive competitors were outflanking it. But contrary to the action required to gain acceptance for the new ideas, the chairman — in order to placate the opposition — promoted prominent spokesmen of the old school into the most visible and highest salaried positions — in particular into three new executive vice presidencies. This meant only one thing to the people in the company: "They don't really mean it." If the greatest rewards are given for behavior contrary to that which the new course of action requires, then everyone will conclude that this is what the people at the top really want and are going to reward.

Only the most effective executive can do what Vail did — build the execution of his decision into the decision itself. But every executive can think through what action commitments a specific decision requires, what work assignments follow from it, and what people are available to carry it out.

The Feedback

Finally, information monitoring and reporting have to be built into the decision to provide continuous testing, against actual events, of the expectations that underlie the decisions. Decisions are made by men. Men are fallible; at best, their works do not last long. Even the best decision has a high probability of being wrong. Even the most effective one eventually becomes obsolete.

This surely needs no documentation. And every executive always builds organized feedback — reports, figures, studies — into his decision to monitor and report on it. Yet far too many decisions fail to achieve their anticipated results, or indeed ever to become effective, despite all these feedback reports. Just as the view from the Matterhorn cannot be visualized by studying a map of Switzerland (one abstraction), a decision cannot be fully and accurately evaluated by studying a report. That is because reports are of necessity abstractions.

Effective decision makers know this and follow a rule which the military developed long ago. The commander who makes a decision does not depend on reports to see how it is being carried out. He — or one of his aides — goes and looks. The reason is not that effective decision makers (or effective commanders) distrust their subordinates. Rather, the reason is that they learned the hard way to distrust abstract "communications."

With the coming of the computer this feedback element will become even more important, for the decision maker will in all likelihood be even further removed from the scene of action. Unless he accepts, as a matter of course, that he had better go out and look at the scene of action, he will be increasingly divorced from reality. All a computer can handle is abstractions. And abstractions can be relied on only if they are constantly checked against concrete results. Otherwise, they are certain to mislead.

To go and look is also the best, if not the only way, for an executive to test whether the assumptions on which his decision has been made are still valid or whether they are becoming obsolete and need to be thought through again. And the executive always has to expect the assumptions to become obsolete sooner or later. Reality never stands still very long.

Failure to go out and look is the typical reason for persisting in a course of action long after it has ceased to be appropriate or even rational. This is true for business decisions as well as for governmental policies. It explains in large measure the failure of Stalin's cold war policy in Europe, but also the inability of the United States to adjust its policies to the realities of a Europe restored to prosperity and economic growth, and the failure of the British to accept, until too late, the reality of the European Common Market. Moreover, in any business I know, failure to go out and look at customers and markets, at competitors and their products, is also a major reason for poor, ineffectual, and wrong decisions.

The decision maker needs organized information for feedback. He needs reports and figures. But unless he builds his feedback around direct exposure to reality — unless he disciplines himself to go out and look — he condemns himself to a sterile dogmatism.

Concluding Note

Decision making is only one of the tasks of an executive. It usually takes but a small fraction of his time. But to make the important decisions is the *specific* executive task. Only an executive makes such decisions.

An *effective* executive makes these decisions as a systematic process with clearly defined elements and in a distinct sequence of steps. Indeed, to be expected (by virtue of position or knowledge) to make decisions that have significant and positive impact on the entire organization, its performance, and its results characterizes the effective executive.

Reprint 67105

THINKING AHEAD

The Big Power of Little Ideas

No artist ever sat down and deliberately
wrote a masterpiece, Somerset Maugham
once pointed out; if he produces a work of art,
it is strictly by chance. But if the
business entrepreneur succeeds, it is not *by*
chance, says Peter F. Drucker;
it is because the small idea his business grew
from not only met the needs of the future,
but shaped the future as well. All
great achievements start with small ideas.
Peter F. Drucker is a management
consultant, lecturer at New York University,
and author of seven books and articles;
two of his HBR articles won the
McKinsey Award for 1962 and 1963.

• THE EDITORS

• Is long-range planning for the big company only?

• Does LRP mean predicting what the future will hold and adapting company actions to the anticipated trends?

Many executives, judging by their actions, would answer *yes* to both these questions. But they are wrong. The correct answer to both is a resounding *no!*

The future cannot be known. The only thing certain about it is that it will be different from, rather than a continuation of, today. But the future is as yet unborn, unformed, undetermined. It can be shaped by purposeful action. And the one thing that can effectively motivate such action is an idea — an idea of a different economy, a different technology, or a different market exploited by a different business.

But ideas always start small. That is why long-range planning is not just for the large company. That is why the small business may actually have an advantage in attempting to shape the future today.

The new, the different, when judged in dollars, always looks so small and insignificant that it tends to be dwarfed by the sheer volume of the existing business in the large company. The few million dollars in sales which a new idea might produce in the next few years, even if wildly successful, look so puny compared to the hundreds of millions the existing businesses of the large company produce that these dollars are sometimes disregarded.

And yet the new requires a great deal of effort. So much so that the small company is often far more willing to tackle the job. This is why there is good reason for the large company to organize special long-range planning effort; otherwise it may never get around to anything but today's work.

But, of course, the small company that does a good job of shaping the future today will not remain a "small business" very long. Every successful large business in existence was once — and often quite recently, as in the case of IBM or Xerox — a small business based on an idea of what the future should be.

This "idea," however, has to be an entrepreneurial one — with potential and capacity for producing wealth — expressed in a going, working, producing business, and effective through business actions and business behavior. Underlying the entrepreneurial idea is always the question: "What major change in economy, market, or knowledge would enable our company to conduct business the way we really would *like* to do it, the way we would really obtain the best economic results?" The dominant question should not be: "What should future society look like?" This is the question of the social reformer, the revolutionary, or the philosopher — not the entrepreneur.

Because this seems so limited, so self-centered an approach, historians have tended to overlook it. They have tended to be oblivious of the impact of the innovat-

ing businessman. The *great* philosophical idea has had, of course, much more profound effects. But, on the other hand, very few philosophical ideas have had any effect at all. And while each business idea is much more limited, larger proportions of them are effective. As a result, innovating businessmen as a group have had a good deal more impact on society than historians realize.

The very fact that theirs are not "big ideas" — ones which encompass all of society or all of knowledge, but "little ideas" which affect just one narrow area — makes the ideas of the entrepreneur much more viable. The people who possess such ideas may be wrong about everything else in the future economy or society. But what does it matter so long as they are approximately right in respect to their own, narrow business focus? All that they need to be successful is just *one* small, specific development. It is true that a few — a very few — big philosophical ideas do become footnotes in history books; however, a great many small entrepreneurial ideas become stock market listings.

* * *

Let us turn to history for some little ideas that have led to large results. First, let us note some ideas from which whole industries grew. (Afterward we will look at some ideas from which great corporations have sprung.)

COMMERCIAL BANKING

The entrepreneurial innovation that has had the greatest impact

was that which converted the theoretical proposition of the French social philosopher, Claude Henri Saint Simon, into a bank a century ago. Saint Simon had started with the concept of the entrepreneur as developed earlier by his compatriot, the economist J. B. Say, to develop a philosophical system around the creative role of capital.

Saint Simon's idea became effective through a banking business: the famous Crédit Mobilier which his disciples, the brothers Pereire, founded in Paris during the middle of the nineteenth century. The Crédit Mobilier was to be the conscious developer of industry through the direction of the liquid resources of the community. It came to be the prototype for the entire banking system of the then "underdeveloped" continent of Europe of the Pereires' days — beginning with France, The Netherlands, and Belgium. The Pereires' imitators then founded the business banks of Germany, Switzerland, Austria, Scandinavia, and Italy, which became the main agents for the industrial development of these countries.

After our Civil War the idea crossed the Atlantic. The U.S. bankers who developed U.S. industry — from Jay Cooke and the American Crédit Mobilier, which financed the transcontinental railroad, to J. P. Morgan — were all imitators of the Pereires, whether they knew it or not. So were the

AUTHOR'S NOTE: This article is adapted from my book, *Managing for Results: Economic Tasks and Risk-Taking Decisions.*

Japanese Zaibatsu — the great banker-industrialists who built the foundations for the economy of modern Japan.

The most faithful disciple of the Pereires, however, has been Soviet Russia. The idea of planning through controlled allocation of capital has been taken directly from the Pereires. There is nothing of this in Marx, above all no planning. All the Soviets actually did was to substitute the state for the individual banker. This was actually a step taken by an Austrian, Rudolf Hilferding, who started out in Vienna as a banker in the business bank tradition and ended as the leading theoretician of German democratic socialism. Hilferding's book, *Finance Capital* (1910), was acknowledged by Lenin to have been the source of his planning and industrialization concepts.

Every single "development bank" started today in an underdeveloped country is still a direct descendant of the original Crédit Mobilier. But the point about the Crédit Mobilier is not that it has had tremendous worldwide impact. The point is that the Pereires started a business — a bank with the intention of making money.

Chemical Industry

By all odds, the modern chemical industry should have arisen in England. In the mid-nineteenth century, England, with its highly developed textile industry, was the major market for chemicals. It also was the home of the scientific leaders of the time — Michael Faraday and Charles Darwin.

The modern chemical industry did actually start with an English discovery: Perkin's discovery of aniline dyes in 1856. Yet 20 years after Perkin's discovery (around 1875) leadership in the new industry had clearly passed to Germany. German businessmen contributed the entrepreneurial idea that was lacking in England: the results of scientific inquiry, organic chemistry in this case, can be directly converted into marketable applications.

Modern Merchandising

The most powerful private business in history was probably managed by the Japanese House of Mitsui, which before its dissolution after World War II was estimated by American occupation authorities to have employed one million people throughout the world. Its origin was the world's first department store, developed in Tokyo during the mid-seventeenth century by an early Mitsui.

The entrepreneurial idea underlying this business was that of the merchant as a principal of economic life, not as a mere middleman. This meant fixed prices to the customer. And it also meant that the Mitsuis no longer acted as agents in dealing with craftsmen and manufacturers. They would buy for their own account and give orders for standardized merchandise to be made according to their specifications. In overseas trade the merchant had acted as a principal all along. However, by 1650 overseas trade had been suppressed in Japan, and the Mitsuis promptly took the overseas-trade concepts and built a domestic merchant-business on them.

Mass Distribution

Great imagination is not necessary to make an entrepreneurial idea successful. All that may be needed is systematic work which will make effective in the future something that has already occurred. Typically, for instance, new developments in the economy and market will run well ahead of distribution. Organizing the distribution, however, may make the change effective — and thereby create a true growth business.

A Canadian, Willard Garfield Weston, saw, for instance, that while the English housewives had come, by the end of World War II, to demand packaged, sliced bread, there was no adequate distribution system to supply them with what they wanted to buy where they wanted to buy it. Because of this small idea one of the largest food-marketing companies in Great Britain was established in a few years.

Today similar distribution opportunities may exist in this country as a result of our massive shift to being a society and economy of "knowledge workers" — that is, people with a high degree of formal education who apply knowledge to work, rather than manual skill or brawn. Education itself is perhaps our biggest and fastest growing market — not only schools and colleges, but also industry with its myriads of training programs, the government, and the armed services.

The office supply market — which delivers whatever the knowledge worker needs to be productive, from paper clips to office reproduction equipment and giant computers — is therefore a major growth market. But while this industry and education are each becoming a true mass market, neither has mass distribution yet. The business that organizes distribution in either market today may well be the Sears, Roebuck of tomorrow.

Discount Chains

The rise of the discount house began in the late 1940's with the application of an idea developed by Sears, Roebuck and Co. almost 20 years earlier. Sears, Roebuck became our leading appliance seller in the 1930's when it began to use a sample of each appliance on the store floor solely to demonstrate the merchandise. The appliance purchased by the customer was delivered straight from the warehouse — which realized savings in costs of uncrating, recrating, and shipping of up to 20% of retail price. Sears, Roebuck made no secret of this; yet there were few imitators of this idea. After World War II there was one small Chicago appliance merchant who adapted the idea to other makers' products. Today Saul Polk is credited with creating the first and largest and one of the most profitable discount chains in existence.

* * *

Little ideas have frequently been the seeds from which giant corporations have grown. Here are a few instances.

IBM

Thomas J. Watson, Jr., who founded and built IBM, did not see the coming development of business technology. But he had the idea of data processing as a unifying concept on which to build a business. IBM was, for a long time, fairly small and confined itself to such mundane work as keeping accounting ledgers and time records. But it was ready to jump when the technology came in — from totally unrelated wartime work — which made data processing by electronic computers actually possible.

While Watson built a small and unspectacular business during the 1920's by designing, selling, and installing punch-card equipment, the logical positivists (e.g., Perry Bridgman in the United States, Rudolph Carnap in Austria) talked and wrote on the systematic methodology of "quantification" and "universal measurements." It is most unlikely that they ever heard of the young, struggling IBM company, and certain that they did not connect their ideas with it. Yet it was Watson's IBM and not their philosophical ideas which became operational when the new technology emerged during World War II.

SEARS, ROEBUCK

The men who built Sears, Roebuck and Co. — Richard Sears, Julius Rosenwald, Albert Loeb, and finally General Robert E. Wood — had active social concerns and lively social imaginations. But not one of them thought of remaking the economy. I doubt that even the idea of a *mass market* — as opposed to the traditional *class market* — occurred to them until long after 1930. From its early beginning, the founders of Sears, Roebuck had the idea that the poor man's money could be made to have the same purchasing power as the rich man's.

But this was not a particularly new idea. Social reformers and economists had bandied it around for decades. The cooperative movement in Europe grew mainly out of it. Sears, Roebuck was, however, the first business in the United States built on this idea. It started with the question: "What would make the farmer a customer for a retail business?" The answer was simple: "He needs to be sure of getting goods of the same dependable quality as do city people but at a low price." In 1900 or even 1920 this was an idea of considerable audacity.

BATA

The basic entrepreneurial idea may be merely an imitation of something that works well in another country or in another industry. For example, when Tomas Bata, the Slovakian shoemaker, returned to Europe from the United States after World War I, he had the idea that everybody in Czechoslovakia and the Balkans could have shoes to wear as did everybody in the United States. "The peasant goes barefoot," he is reported to have said, "not because he is too poor, but because there are no shoes." What was needed to make this vision of a shod peasant come true was someone supplying him with cheap, standardized, but well-designed and durable footwear as was done in the United States.

On the basis of this analogy with America, Bata began without capital in a rented shack and in a few years built pre-Nazi Europe's largest shoe business and one of Europe's most successful companies. Yet to apply U.S. mass-production methods to European consumer goods was hardly a very original idea in the 1920's when Henry Ford and his assembly line were all the rage in Europe. The only original thing was willingness to act on the idea.

*   *   *

To make the future happen requires work rather than "genius." The man with a creative imagination will have more imaginative ideas, to be sure. But whether the more imaginative ideas will actually turn out to be more successful is by no means certain.

Creativity, which looms so large in present discussions of innovation, is not the real problem. There are usually more ideas in any organization, including businesses, than can possibly be put to use.[1] Ask any company — including seemingly moribund ones — this question: "What in our economy, or our society, or our state of knowledge would give our business its greatest opportunity if only we could make it happen?" Dozens of responses will burst from management's lips. As a rule we are not lacking *ideas* — not even good, serviceable ideas. What is lacking is management's *willingness to welcome ideas*, in fact, solicit them, rather than just products or processes. Products and processes, after all, are only the vehicles through which the ideas become effective. The specific future products and processes often cannot even be imagined.

For example, when Du Pont started the work on polymer chemistry out of which nylon eventually evolved, it did not know that man-made fibers would be the end-product. Du Pont acted on the assumption that any gain in man's ability to manipulate the structure of large, organic molecules — a scientific skill at that time in its infancy — would lead to commercially important results of some kind. It was only after six or seven years of research work that man-made fibers first appeared as a possible major result area.

Indeed, as the IBM experience shows, the specific products and processes that make an idea truly successful often come out of entirely different and unrelated work.

But there must always be a willingness to think in terms of the general rather than the specific, in terms of a business, the contributions it makes, the satisfactions it supplies, the market and economy it serves. This is the entrepreneurial point of view. And it is accessible to the average businessman.

Also, the manager must have the courage to commit resources — and in particular first-rate peo-

[1] See Theodore Levitt, "Creativity Is Not Enough," HBR May–June 1963, p. 72.

ple — to work on making the future happen. The staffs for this work should be small. But they should contain the very best men available; otherwise, nothing will happen.

*   *   *

The businessman needs a touchstone of validity and practicality for entrepreneurial, future-making ideas. Indeed, the reason some businesses fail to innovate is not that they shy away from ideas. It is that they engage in hopelessly romantic ones — at great cost in men and money. An idea must meet rigorous tests of practicality if it is to be capable of making a business successful in the future.

It must first have operational validity. Can we take action on this idea? Or can we only talk about it? Can we really do something right away to bring about the kind of future we desire? Sears, Roebuck, with its idea of bringing the market to the isolated U.S. farmer, could show immediate results. In contrast, Du Pont with its idea of polymer chemistry could only organize research work on a very small scale. It could only underwrite the research of one first-rate man. But both companies could *do* something right away.

To be able to spend money on research is not enough. It must be research directed toward the realization of the idea. The knowledge sought may be general — as was that of Du Pont's project. But it must be reasonably clear, at least, that, if available, the knowledge gained will be applicable to operations.

The idea must have economic validity. If it could be put to work immediately, it would have to be able to produce economic results. We may not be able to do *all* that we would like to see done — not for a long time, and perhaps never. But if we could do something right away, the resulting products, processes, or services would find a customer, a market, an end use, and would be capable of being sold profitably. In short, they should satisfy a want and need.

Finally, the idea must meet the test of personal commitment. Do we really believe in the idea? Do we really want to be that kind of people, do that kind of work, run that kind of business?

To make the future demands courage. It demands work. But it also demands faith. To commit oneself to the expedient is simply not practical. It will not suffice for the trials ahead. For no such idea is foolproof — nor should it be.

The one idea about the future that *must* fail is the apparently sure thing, the riskless idea, which is believed to be incapable of failure. The ideas on which tomorrow's business is to be built *must* be uncertain; no one can really say, as yet, what they will look like if and when they become reality. They *must* be risky; they have a probability of success, of course, but also a probability of failure. If they are not both uncertain and risky, they are simply not practical ideas for the future.

Conclusion

It is not absolutely necessary for every business to search for the idea that will make the future, and to start work on its realization. Indeed, a good many managements do not even make their present business effective — and yet their company somehow survives for a while. Big businesses, in particular, seem able to coast a long time on the courage, work, and vision of earlier executives before they erode and run down.

But the future always does come, sooner or later. And it is always different. Even the mightiest company will be in trouble if it does not work toward the future. It will lose distinction and leadership. All that will be left is big-company overhead. It will neither control nor understand what is happening.

By not daring to take the risk of making the new happen, management takes, by default, the greater risk of being surprised by what will happen. This is a risk that even the largest and richest company cannot afford to take. And it is a risk that not even the smallest company need take.

— *Peter F. Drucker*

Reprint 64303

CUSTOM PUBLICATIONS • BOOKS • ARTICLES • VIDEOS • CUSTOM PUBLICATIONS • BOOKS • ARTICLES • VIDEOS • BOOKS •

READ THE FINE PRINT

REPRINTS
Telephone: 617-495-6192
Fax: 617-495-6985

Current and past articles are available, as is an annually updated index. Discounts apply to large-quantity purchases.

Please send orders to
HBR Reprints
Harvard Business School
Publishing Division
Boston, MA 02163.

HOW CAN *HARVARD BUSINESS REVIEW* ARTICLES WORK FOR YOU?

For years, we've printed a microscopically small notice on the editorial credits page of the *Harvard Business Review* alerting our readers to the availability of *HBR* articles.

Now we invite you to take a closer look at some of the many ways you can put this hard-working business tool to work for you.

IN THE CORPORATE CLASSROOM.

There's no more effective, or cost-effective, way to supplement your corporate training programs than in-depth, incisive *HBR* articles.

Affordable and accessible, it's no wonder hundreds of companies and consulting organizations use *HBR* articles as a centerpiece for management training.

IN-BOX INNOVATION.

Where do your company's movers and shakers get their big ideas? Many find the inspiration for innovation in the pages of *HBR*. They then share the wealth and spread the word by distributing *HBR* articles to company colleagues.

IN MARKETING AND SALES SUPPORT.

HBR articles are a substantive leave-behind to your sales calls. And they can add credibility to your direct mail campaigns. They demonstrate that your company is on the leading edge of business thinking.

CREATE CUSTOM ARTICLES.

If you want to pack even greater power in your punch, personalize *HBR* articles with your company's name or logo. And get the added benefit of putting your organization's name before your customers.

AND THERE ARE 500 MORE REASONS IN THE *HBR CATALOG.*

In all, the *Harvard Business Review Catalog* lists articles on over 500 different subjects. Plus, you'll find books and videos on subjects you need to know.

The catalog is yours for just $8.00. To order *HBR* articles or the *HBR Catalog* (No. 21019), call 617-495-6192. Please mention telephone order code 025A when placing your order. Or FAX us at 617-495-6985.

And start putting *HBR* articles to work for you.

**Harvard Business School
Publications**

Call 617-495-6192 to order the *HBR Catalog.*

(Prices and terms subject to change.)

BOOKS • CUSTOM PUBLICATIONS • ARTICLES • VIDEOS • CUSTOM PUBLICATIONS • BOOKS • ARTICLES • VIDEOS • BOOKS

CUSTOM PUBLICATIONS • BOOKS • ARTICLES • VIDEOS • CASES • CUSTOM PUBLICATIONS • BOOKS • ARTICLES • VIDEOS

YOU SAID: AND WE SAID:

"Give us training tools that are relevant to our business...ones we can use *now.*"

"We need new cases that stimulate meaningful discussion."

"It can't be a catalog of canned programs... everything we do is custom."

"Make it a single source for up-to-date materials ...on the most current business topics."

"Better yet if it's from a reputable business school. That adds credibility."

"Introducing the Harvard Business School Publications Corporate Training and Development Catalog."

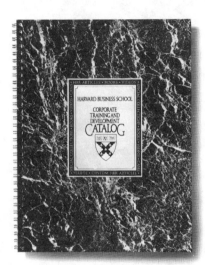

You asked for it. And now it's here.

The Harvard Business School Publications Corporate Training and Development Catalog is created exclusively for those who design and develop custom training programs.

It's filled cover-to-cover with valuable materials you can put to work on the spot. You'll find a comprehensive selection of cases, *Harvard Business Review* articles, videos, books, and more.

Our new catalog covers the critical management topics affecting corporations today, like Leadership, Quality, Global Business, Marketing, and Strategy, to name a few. And it's all organized, indexed, and cross-referenced to make it easy for you to find precisely what you need.

Harvard Business School Publications

HOW TO ORDER.

To order by FAX, dial 617-495-6985. Or call 617-495-6192. Please mention telephone order code 132A. Or send this coupon with your credit card information to: HBS Publications Corporate Training and Development Catalog, Harvard Business School Publishing Division, Operations Department, Boston, MA 02163. **All orders must be prepaid.**

Order No.	Title	Qty. ×	Price +	Shipping* =	Total
39001	Catalog		$8		

Prices and terms subject to change.
*For orders outside Continental U.S.: 20% for surface delivery. Allow 3-6 months. *Express Deliveries* billed at cost; all foreign orders not designating express delivery will be sent by surface mail.

☐ VISA   ☐ American Express   ☐ MasterCard

Card Number_____ Exp. Date_____

Signature_____

Telephone_____ FAX_____

Name_____

Organization_____

Street_____

City_____ State/Zip_____

Country_____ ☐ Home Address   ☐ Organization Address

Please Reference Telephone Order Code 132A

ARTICLES • BOOKS • CUSTOM PUBLICATIONS • VIDEOS • CASES • CUSTOM PUBLICATIONS • BOOKS • ARTICLES • VIDEOS •